BRAVEST OF THE BRAVE

ADVANCE PRAISE FOR THE BOOK

Lt Gen. Satish Dua has served extensively in the erstwhile state of Jammu and Kashmir (J&K) and also belongs to the Jammu and Kashmir Light Infantry (JAKLI), a regiment that comprises sons of the soil from that region. He has been deployed in different parts of J&K and ended up as the Corps Commander of Kashmir, a post with onerous national responsibilities that I also held some years before him. Like his previous books, he yet again writes about the bravery of the soldiers from his regiment—the JAKLI.

Lt Gen. Dua's narrative brings to life the combat environment at the LoC and counter-terrorist operations in J&K in a manner that the reader feels a personal involvement in them, more so as the book also vividly portrays the emotions that soldiers undergo in such operations, with threat to life everywhere. I am confident that this book will motivate and inspire many who admire the Indian Army's fortitude, valour and patriotism.

—Lt Gen. Syed Ata Hasnain (Retd),
Former Corps Commander in Kashmir

Lt Gen. Satish Dua is an accomplished soldier-narrator. One of the most respected and regarded military leaders, he is a soldiers' General. For the better part of his service, he has been deployed in the operational areas of Jammu and Kashmir. He belongs to the Jammu and Kashmir Light Infantry Regiment, which has soldiers only from the erstwhile state of Jammu and Kashmir. His understanding of the bravery of these sons of the soil and the nuances of the regional dynamics is comprehensive. This is his third book on the subject.

Lt Gen. Dua's narrative is simple yet powerful. It portrays the valour of the brave soldiers, harshness of the terrain and climate and the range of emotions that run through the minds of soldiers in combat. This book will captivate and motivate the reader and is sure to inspire future generations as he captures the never-say-die spirit of soldiers like Chunni Lal.

—Lt Gen. Vinod Bhatia (Retd),
Former Director General of Military Operations

Lt Gen. Satish Dua and I have had the privilege of serving together in Jammu and Kashmir on more occasions than one. I can say, therefore, with complete certitude and honesty, that when it comes to sheer operational situations/challenges, there are few as authentic as him. Cool as a cucumber, decisive to the core, operationally vibrant, he thinks on his feet and leads by example. *An outstanding combat leader with a rare talent for operations and war.*

This book is fascinating. The author's unique style—a simple, gripping narration shorn of high-sounding rhetoric—makes it even more compelling.

Welcome to the life and times of Chunni Lal and the rarefied environs of the Indian Army, where valour is a tradition and gallantry a way of life.

—Lt Gen. Raj Shukla (Retd),
Former GOC-in-C, Army Training Command

BRAVEST OF THE BRAVE

THE INSPIRING STORY OF
NAIB SUBEDAR CHUNNI LAL, AC, VrC, SM

LT GEN. SATISH DUA

HarperCollins *Publishers* India

First published in India by HarperCollins *Publishers* 2025
HarperCollins *Publishers* India, Cyber City,
Building 10-A, Gurugram, Haryana-122002, India
www.harpercollins.co.in

2 4 6 8 10 9 7 5 3 1

Copyright © Lt Gen. Satish Dua (Retd) 2025

P-ISBN: 978-93-6989-452-9
E-ISBN: 978-93-6989-664-6

The views and opinions expressed in this book are the author's own
and the facts are as reported by him, and the publishers
are not in any way liable for the same.

Lt Gen. Satish Dua (Retd) asserts the moral right
to be identified as the author of this work.

All rights reserved. No part of this publication may be reproduced,
stored in a retrieval system, or transmitted, in any form or by any means,
electronic, mechanical, photocopying, recording or otherwise,
without the prior permission of the publishers.

Without limiting the exclusive rights of any author, contributor or
the publisher of this publication, any unauthorized use of this publication
to train generative artificial intelligence (AI) technologies is expressly
prohibited. HarperCollins also exercise their rights under Article 4(3) of
the Digital Single Market Directive 2019/790 and expressly reserve this
publication from the text and data-mining exception.

Typeset in 11.5/16.3 Adobe Garamond Pro
by HarperCollins *Publishers* India Pvt. Ltd

Printed and bound at
Thomson Press (India) Ltd.

This book is produced from independently certified FSC® paper
to ensure responsible forest management.

HarperCollins *Publishers*, Macken House, 39/40 Mayor Street Upper,
Dublin 1, D01 C9W8, Ireland

To the brave Indian Soldier, who asks for so little, and yet is always willing and ready to risk his life for the country

Contents

Foreword by Chief of the Army Staff	xiii
Preface	xvii
Glossary	xxi
1. Chunni Lal: The Bravest of the Brave	1
2. A Dream of Soldiering Marches On: Chunni Lal Wears the Uniform	9
3. 'I Am a Soldier'	33
4. Bravery on Top: Induction into the Siachen Glacier	41
5. Frozen and Skyward: The Highest Attack in the World	49
6. Attack Aftermath at the Siachen	86
7. Of Peace Around the World: Chunni Lal Goes on a Global UN Mission	100
8. Golden Jubilee Tenure	111
9. The Tathawade Operation	144

10. An Eternal Stamp of Bravery: The Vir Chakra	155
11. *Voh Dekh Raha Hai*	175
12. Global Peacekeeping Round II: Sudan and Onwards	180
13. The Last Operation	189
Afterword	205
Acknowledgements	209
Notes	211

Foreword

MESSAGE

It is with a sense of honour and reverence that I write this Foreword for a book that chronicles the life and bravery of one of the most distinguished soldiers of the Indian Army – Naib Subedar Chunni Lal, AC, VrC, SM. Lt Gen Satish Dua, PVSM, UYSM, SM, VSM (Retd) is perhaps the most apt person to capture the essence of the decorated soldier's life, since the two belong to the same battalion – 8 Jammu & Kashmir Light Infantry (Siachen).

The author has vividly portrayed the life journey of the soldier, from his humble beginning in the Bhaderwah region in Jammu & Kashmir to becoming an exemplar of fortitude, courage and sacrifice. Through precise descriptions and meticulous details, the leaves of the book capture the intensity of each battle and encounter where the fearless actions of Naib Subedar Chunni Lal came to the fore. These span from the icy heights of Siachen Glacier, to the counter terror operations and Line of Control in Jammu & Kashmir. In doing so, the author not only pays a rich tribute to the brave soldier, but also underscores the larger ethos of Indian Army, that stands on the edifice of 'Naam', 'Namak' aur 'Nishan'.

The powerful legacy of Naib Subedar Chunni Lal, encapsulated in the book, will inspire not only serving soldiers, but future generations also, especially those who nurture a dream to don the uniform one day.

My compliments to Lt Gen Gen Satish Dua for presenting the life canvas of a brave soldier, in the depth and respect it deserves. I wish him success in his future endeavours too.

'Jai Hind'

(Upendra Dwivedi)
General
Chief of the Army Staff

Message

It is with a sense of honour and reverence that I write this Foreword for a book that chronicles the life and bravery of one of the most distinguished soldiers of the Indian Army—Naib Subedar Chunni Lal, AC, VrC, SM. Lt Gen. Satish Dua, PVSM, UYSM, SM, VSM (Retd), is perhaps the most apt person to capture the essence of the decorated soldier's life, since the two belong to the same battalion—8 Jammu & Kashmir Light Infantry (Siachen).

The author has vividly portrayed the life journey of the soldier, from his humble beginning in the Bhaderwah region in Jammu & Kashmir to becoming an exemplar of fortitude, courage and sacrifice. Through precise descriptions and meticulous details, the leaves of the book capture the intensity of each battle and encounter where the fearless actions of Naib Subedar Chunni Lal came to the fore. These span from the icy heights of [the] Siachen Glacier to the counter-terror operations and Line of Control in Jammu & Kashmir. In doing so, the author not only pays a rich tribute to the brave soldier but also underscores the larger ethos of Indian Army, that stands on the edifice of 'Naam', 'Namak' aur 'Nishan'.

The powerful legacy of Naib Subedar Chunni Lal, encapsulated in the book, will inspire not only serving soldiers but future generations also, especially those who nurture a dream to don the uniform one day.

My compliments to Lt Gen. Satish Dua for presenting the life canvas of a brave soldier, in the depth and respect it deserves. I wish him success in his future endeavours too.

'Jai Hind'

Upendra Dwivedi
General
Chief of the Army Staff

Preface

*I*T WAS YET *another day at Siachen—frozen, isolated and cut off. An artillery shell exploded, which made the enemy duck for safety and stay hidden for some time. Taking advantage of this, Chunni and Laxman darted across. They crossed the bunker that had been captured, also crossing over a few bodies of our fallen soldiers. They reached close to the enemy bunker. It was eerily quiet for a bit. Chunni prepared to lob a grenade inside. He crawled very close to the bunker, pulled the pin out with his mouth, released the lever and held the grenade in his hand for a second, and then pushed it carefully inside the bunker. This way the grenade had only two seconds to explode. No time for the enemy to throw it back. And their prayers were answered. There was a loud explosion inside the bunker, though muffled. They heard cries of Pakistani soldiers: 'Yah Allah'. (We will read more about this operation in detail later in the book.)*

I first heard of Rifleman (Rfn) Chunni Lal when he was already a hero. In 1987, during the highest attack in the world at the Siachen

Glacier, he was the first to reach the enemy post. He was a part of Naib Subedar (Nb Sub.) Bana Singh's section that led the attack to capture the enemy post. The post was subsequently named 'Bana Top' in honour of the section commander, who was awarded the Param Vir Chakra (PVC). Rifleman Chunni Lal was awarded the Sena Medal (SM). He was barely nineteen. All the other members of the section were also awarded either the Vir Chakra (VrC) or the SM.

As a rookie soldier, Chunni had displayed fearlessness and raw courage that left everyone dumbfounded. The start of his career as a nineteen-year-old soldier was literally baptized by fire. As a soldier, from thereon he grew up among heroes. Over the years, he turned out to be the biggest hero of them all. At 5 feet 3 inches, Chunni Lal stood mighty tall. This is his story.

I am fortunate that we are from the same battalion. When I became the Commanding Officer (CO) of the battalion at the Line of Control (LoC—an unresolved border between India and Pakistan in Jammu and Kashmir) a decade later, Chunni was a combat-experienced Havildar (Hav.). I was fortunate to participate in numerous combat situations with an inspirational junior leader like him. Not only was he an inspirational figure for the younger soldiers, but he was also a reassuring factor for his superiors. His mere presence in a combat situation made me rest easy as a CO.

'When Chunni is there, there is no reason to worry. He will take care of things, and we will come out victorious'—he had come to be considered that kind of good-luck charm for the battalion. He displayed nerves of steel, as the reader will read in this book. He was awarded the Vir Chakra (VrC) during my command tenure at the LoC.

Seven years later, on 24 June 2007, again deployed on the LoC in Kupwara District, North Kashmir, in a counter-infiltration operation,

Chunni Lal, now a Naib Subedar, bravely foiled a big infiltration attempt by terrorists, laying down his life in the firefight. He was posthumously awarded the highest peacetime gallantry award, the Ashok Chakra, by a grateful nation in recognition of his undaunted valour and his supreme sacrifice. With this Ashok Chakra, and having already been awarded the Vir Chakra and the Sena Medal, Nb Sub. Chunni Lal, AC, VrC, SM, became the only soldier in the Indian Army to be awarded three out of the nation's top four gallantry awards. His name figures in the *Limca Book of Records* for this.

Not only did he set a benchmark in combat, but this legendary soldier also went on to serve twice in United Nations (UN) peacekeeping missions abroad, and also served as an instructor at the Officers Training Academy (OTA) in Kamptee, Maharashtra.

Chunni was a great human being, as kind to fellow humans as he was viciously violent to the enemy. A decade after his death, I went to his village in a remote mountainous region of (the then state of) Jammu and Kashmir (J&K) to attend his daughter's wedding. One year after my retirement, I made a motorbike trip to his home in the mountains to inaugurate a bust of Chunni Lal installed in a park named after him. Such are the bonds of brotherhood among soldiers.

All Indian Army soldiers are brave, but Chunni stood out as one of the bravest. This humble son of a modest farmer grew up to be the bravest of the brave soldiers, a legendary figure, a dutiful son, a loving husband, a doting father and a dedicated son of Mother India.

This is his story.

Jai Hind.

As a rookie soldier, Chunni had displayed fearlessness and raw courage that left everyone dumbfounded. The start of his career as a nineteen-year-old soldier was literally baptized by fire. As a soldier, from thereon he grew up among heroes. Over the years, he turned out to be the biggest hero of them all. At 5 feet 3 inches, Chunni Lal stood mighty tall. This is his story.

Glossary

Indian Army All Ranks
Officers

Lieutenant General	Lt Gen; addressed as General
Major General	Maj. Gen; addressed as General
Brigadier	Brig.
Colonel	Col
Lieutenant Colonel	Lt Col; addressed as Colonel
Major	Maj.
Captain	Capt.
Lieutenant	Lt
Second Lieutenant	2 Lt; addressed as Lieutenant

Junior Commissioned Officers (JCOs)

Subedar Major	Sub. Maj.; often addressed as SM Saheb
Subedar	Sub.
Naib Subedar	Nb Sub

Non-Commissioned Officers (NCOs)

Company Havildar Major	CHM
Company Quarter Master Havildar	CQMH
Havildar	Hav.
Naik	Nk
Lance Naik	L/Nk

Other Terms

JAKLI	Jammu and Kashmir Light Infantry
RR	Rashtriya Rifles
Bn	Battalion
COB	Company Operating Base
JCO	Junior Commissioned Officer
NCO	Non-Commissioned Officer
POK	Pakistan Occupied Kashmir
LoC	Line of Control

Glossary

BAT	Border Action Team
BIT	Brigade Intelligence Team
FT	Foreign terrorists
UBGL	Under Barrel Grenade Launcher
MMG	Medium Machine Gun
LMG	Light Machine Gun
BPP	Bulletproof Patka
QRT	Quick Reaction Team
UAV	Unarmed Aerial Vehicles
IED	Improvised Explosive Device
HAPO	High Altitude Pulmonary Oedema

1

Chunni Lal
The Bravest of the Brave

It was a cold winter morning. January is always very cold in Delhi. But it was a vibrant day, full of energy. It was the morning of Republic Day in the year 2008. At Rajpath (now renovated and called Kartavya Path), the crowds were braving the cold, waiting for the Republic Day Parade to start. Suddenly, the clip-clop of horses' hooves was heard over the buzz of conversations and announcements over the public address system. It was the President's Bodyguard escorting the President towards the dais. President Pratibha Patil was not alone. President Nicolas Sarkozy of France, who was the chief guest, accompanied the President of India. They were received by the Prime Minister, the Defence Minister, the Chiefs of the Indian Army, Navy and Air Force and the Defence Secretary.

The President's Bodyguard troop saluted in the ceremonial cavalry style as they took leave. It was an impressive sight. The two Presidents mounted the steps leading to the dais escorted by others, as the announcer could be heard announcing the arrival of the two

Presidents. As soon as the dignitaries were seated, the first activity—honouring the Bravehearts, including those who had made the supreme sacrifice in the service of the nation—began.

The announcer read out, 'Naib Subedar Chunni Lal, Vir Chakra, Sena Medal, Jammu and Kashmir Light Infantry (Posthumous).'

She paused. The cameras focused on his widow, Smt. Chinta Devi. She was escorted by the CO of the unit, Colonel (Col) R.P. Singh. They both started walking up the steps of the dais. The cameras also focused briefly on her children, one boy and two girls, who were seated in the VIP stands.

The announcer continued, 'On 24th June 2007, Naib Subedar Chunni Lal, Vir Chakra, Sena Medal, was deployed on the Line of Control in Kashmir. He received information about a group of infiltrating terrorists—'

As the Colonel and the soldier's widow reached the dais, the President stood up and folded her hands. Srimati Chinta Devi also folded her hands, and Nb Sub. Chunni Lal's CO saluted. Everyone fell silent. It was a sombre moment.

The announcer was reading the citation:

... Realizing the likelihood of terrorists' escape and threat to the 'lives'? of soldiers, Naib Subedar Chunni Lal, Vir Chakra, Sena Medal, in a death-defying act, charged at the terrorists, killing one of them instantly and surprising the rest. He also evacuated two of his wounded comrades, thus saving their lives. Fierce exchange of fire ensued between him and the terrorists, in which he bravely eliminated two more terrorists. However, he sustained multiple gunshot wounds. Bleeding profusely, he continued to fire at the terrorists, blocking their escape routes, which ultimately resulted in the elimination of five hardcore terrorists and saving the lives of several soldiers. He, however, succumbed to his wounds on the spot. For displaying unparalleled bravery and supreme sacrifice in the line of duty, Nb Sub. Chunni Lal, Vir Chakra, Sena Medal, is awarded the Ashok Chakra (Posthumous).

Although a difficult thing to achieve in large crowds, there was pin-drop silence, as if no one wanted to miss even a single word. It was overwhelming. It was even more poignant to look at the gaunt face of Smt. Chinta Devi, the widow of the fallen hero. There was not a tear in her eyes, and yet, there wasn't a dry eye in the crowd.

Hundreds of kilometres to the north, in the remote village of Bhaderwah in J&K, Shanker Dass and his wife, Shakuntla Devi, had tears in their eyes as they watched on television their brave son being awarded the nation's highest gallantry medal posthumously. Little did they realize that their son had gone into the annals of military history as the most decorated soldier in the Indian Army. No one individual soldier had been awarded these three gallantry medals before—the Ashok Chakra, the Vir Chakra and the Sena Medal.

His mother, with tears in her eyes and a heavy heart, recalled that Chunni was such a quiet child when he was born. He did not cry much and never disturbed her sleep much at night, unlike his younger siblings. He had been rather quiet and unassuming all his life. He let his actions speak louder than his words. Thinking of her eldest son, Chunni, she couldn't help recalling that whenever she told him to wear better clothes, he would say, 'Clothes don't make a man.' Chunni had very simple habits, she remembered with pride and affection. Oh God, she would never see him again. The stream of tears flowed unceasingly down her cheeks as she sobbed loudly. More than half a year had elapsed since his passing, yet her heart was still full of anguish. It struck her again, as it had many times in the past many months, that she would never see her son again. A mother's heart felt his absence more than the pride of the medals.

His father's heart was filled with grief, but it also swelled with pride. Shanker Dass remembered the day when he enrolled into the army. His son had returned home from Doda after getting selected and had informed him with a mixture of pride and simplicity. 'I am going to become a good soldier,' he had said. 'I need your blessings, Father.'

'Be brave; be a good soldier,' his father had replied. 'God bless.'

Shanker also recalled with great pride how brave he had always been. His son's milestones in the Army stood out in his memory. As a young soldier with less than three years in service, he participated in an attack on enemy troops in the Siachen Glacier, the highest battlefield in the world. He was one of the youngest to be awarded the Sena Medal, the nation's fourth-highest gallantry award. Several years later, as a Havildar, he participated in several operations on the LoC and was awarded the Vir Chakra, the nation's third-highest gallantry medal. Shanker's chest swelled with pride when he saw the photograph of his son receiving the Vir Chakra Medal from the President of India. He became a hero of the village. Even the local Member of the Legislative Assembly (MLA) had sent his greetings through the numberdar of his village.

In 2007, Chunni laid down his life while fighting for the country, exactly twenty years after the operation for which he got the Sena Medal. When his colleagues Suresh and others brought his body home, he was given a hero's farewell by the villagers and a ceremonial salute by the army. The whole village had turned up. The Rashtriya Rifles Battalion Guard found it difficult to maintain order while acquitting the ceremonial part of the farewell.

Shanker's eyes brimmed over with tears as he watched the President on television giving the Ashok Chakra medal to his daughter-in-law. Unable to control his grief, he cried out, 'Oh, my son, Oh my brave son—' This bereaved father had once said, 'My one son will do what a hundred other sons put together cannot do.'

Chunni's family, his relatives and friends all watched the ceremony on television. Many of them came over to Shanker Dass' home that afternoon. People kept coming and going that afternoon and evening. Everyone felt proud of this son of the soil. They all paid their respects to the Braveheart and to the family. Chunni's parents were overwhelmed with pride, but it also refreshed the grief.

By the time darkness fell, everyone had left except the family. Shanker's younger son Pyara Lal and his children were also quiet. The mood was sombre. There were too many memories. Sitting alone for some time, Shanker reminisced that when Chunni was born nearly four decades ago, they did not live in this house but in Paddar, beyond Kishtwar. That area was very remote and backward. When Chunni was a year old, Shanker moved the family to Bhaderwah, bought some land and settled in Bhara Village, where he built his present abode. Chunni's siblings, two brothers and four sisters, were born here. Shanker had modest landholdings, but he had brought up his children with good values of honesty and patriotism.

It was a tradition in the villages to send one son to the army, and Shanker had given one brave son to the country who was equal to many. He recalled that after Chunni returned from serving abroad in Sudan, he had asked him to retire and take care of his family. Chunni's reply had been that the army was his life and he could not think of any other way to live. In a way, Chunni had fulfilled his own dream.

Neither Shanker nor Shakuntala had much appetite for dinner that day, as their hearts were full. 'My heart is so full of grief today that I cannot sleep,' said Chunni's mother.

'Yes, you're right,' said his father, 'today's ceremony in Delhi has opened up old wounds, just when we had learnt to dry our eyes since his passing away last year. But we must also remember that not only our village but also the whole country is saying today that we are the proud parents of a hero who was the braves of the brave. He has attained what no one has. You are the great mother who gave birth to such a hero.'

On the television, the announcer had finished reading out the citation. She announced one more time, 'Mrs Chinta Devi.' Their daughter-in-law received the Ashok Chakra and the parchment from the President and folded her hands once again. Colonel R.P. Singh saluted and escorted their daughter-in-law back to her seat, where her children were seated too. She handed over the medal and parchment to her son, who looked at both with awe before handing them over to his sisters seated next to him. His mother held her son's hand tightly. No words were exchanged.

The Republic Day Parade started. This was the first time that Chunni's wife and children were seeing the Parade at the venue. The children soon got engrossed, but Chinta Devi's mind was far away. Her thoughts went to the last time she had seen her husband. Then, unbidden, she also recalled the first time she had seen him, when he had come with his parents to fix their wedding. She had felt so shy that she could barely peek through the dupatta that nearly covered her face. Her mind strayed to their wedding, when Chunni had looked so handsome, dressed as a bridegroom.

For some reason, Chunni's teenage son, Manveer, could not get his mind off a few lines of a battalion song that his father used to hum to him often:

> *Vir to hum mein char hue,*
> *Ab Param ka chakkar pana hai.*
> *Agla mauka milne par,*
> *Seene pe ise lagana hai.*
> *(Four of our soldiers have so far been awarded the Vir Chakra,*
> *Now we have to attain the Param Vir Chakra.*
> *On the next possible opportunity,*
> *We have to pin it to our chest.)*[1]

His father had finally been awarded the peacetime equivalent of the Param Vir Chakra, but at a great price. He could not wait to follow in his footsteps and join the Indian Army, join his father's 'Bravest of the Brave Battalion'—8 JAKLI (Siachen).

It was a tradition in the villages to send one son to the army, and Shanker had given one brave son to the country who was equal to many. He recalled that after Chunni returned from serving abroad in Sudan, he had asked him to retire and take care of his family. Chunni's reply had been that Army was his life and he could not think of any other way to live. In a way, Chunni had fulfilled his own dream.

2

A Dream of Soldiering Marches On
Chunni Lal Wears the Uniform

IN HIS YOUNGER years, faujis were Chunni's role models. He had seen many in his village—newly recruited, retired, on duty and those spending some quality time with family while on leave. They brought their stories with them, and young Chunni sat enveloped in them. He would be spellbound as these soldiers regaled him with tales of wars, grit and, above all, camaraderie—which impressed Chunni the most. He would marvel at the ease with which these jawans braved tough conditions and went on missions with tremendous courage. These stories of bravery made him proud. They built in him the determination to serve his nation. He lived his promise right till the end of his life, which ended in a sacrifice that no words can surmise.

The First Step

An Army recruitment rally was being held in the neighbouring district of Doda in the mountainous region of the erstwhile state of Jammu and Kashmir (J&K is now a union territory that no longer includes Ladakh). Chunni and a few other boys from near his village went for recruitment on the appointed day. They left home a day early and Chunni spent the night at a distant relative's house, who was living without his family in Doda town because of his job.

On the day of the recruitment, they reached the venue early in the morning. A huge crowd had turned up for recruitment; some boys were also accompanied by their fathers, most of whom were retired soldiers. You could tell by their demeanour. That is the best part about the army—a soldier stands out even after retirement.

They were made to pass under a low gate that had been erected for the purpose. They had to bow their heads to pass under it. Chunni knew that it was a height test. Anyone shorter than 5 feet, one inch would not have to bow his head but would have to bow out of the recruitment tests. Chunni was unnecessarily anxious about this because of his height, though at 5 feet and 3 inches he was clearly above the qualifying mark. Somehow that anxiety stayed until he passed through the gate, bowing his head as if in a silent prayer of thanks to God. He was confident about the rest of the tests.

The first test was a one-mile run, which they had to complete in six minutes. Most boys get eliminated in this test. But not Chunni. He was far ahead of the cut-off point. Many boys were panting hard after completing the run, one was also retching. Chunni was totally at ease with himself. He also did not have any trouble passing the other physical tests, like chin-ups and jumping across a nine-foot ditch. A tough and determined mountain lad, he had been preparing for this. Climbing up and down the mountains all his life had given him a strong pair of legs.

He was then sent for a medical check-up. He did not anticipate any problem in medicals, now that he had cleared the height bar in the beginning itself.

During a break at a tea shop, he met another young man around his age named Suresh, who was a local of Doda District itself. He had also cleared all the tests. They were going to be together during their training at the Jammu and Kashmir Light Infantry (JAKLI) Regimental Training Centre, as this was a JAKLI Regiment recruitment. Another young lad joined them and said, 'I can make out you two are celebrating being selected. I'm Narad, also selected, so we're going to be soldiers together. Here's to friendship.'

'Only if you don't live up to your name,' muttered Chunni. They all laughed.

Training Begins

Chunni, Suresh and Narad became good friends during training and were fortunate to be allotted to the same battalion after training—8 JAKLI. A regiment has a number of battalions but a common regimental training centre. JAKLI had nine battalions in those days, and the JAKLI Training Centre was in Srinagar. Chunni had never been to Srinagar and was excited at the prospect of going there.

The trio travelled together and reported at the training centre in Srinagar on the appointed date. The neat rows of barracks, the straight grass-lined roads and the soldiers and recruits marching from one place to the other in squads of four or six instead of slouching singly were very impressive.

Soon, all the recruits gathered at a small Parade ground, and a Havildar with a big moustache addressed them. He made them stand in three columns and said, 'You all probably think you are heroes just because you got selected to join the army. You are not heroes—you are zeros. You are zeros as soldiers. My team and I, Hav. Mohammad Sher Khan, will make you soldiers, and to make you good soldiers will not be easy. Be prepared for a lot of physical and mental stress. If you find it too tough and want to leave, be a man first and report to me or your Platoon Havildar about your disenchantment; don't run away in the night like a coward.' He glared at all the faces as if to spot prospective deserters, and while many looked down, Chunni held his gaze and their eyes met fleetingly. Chunni felt as though an electric current had passed from the instructor to him.

The Havildar continued, 'Our first job is to make men out of you boys, and by God, we will do it.' He paused for effect, then continued, 'First rule and most important—during training, your HI, that is, your Havildar Instructor, is your God. Follow him blindly, obey him blindly. Second rule—never be late anywhere, even if it is raining or snowing; remember, in war, the enemy will not wait for good weather. So get wet if you have to, but never be late. For anything, even a movie.'

Before being taken to the barracks, they were divided into sections and platoons. A section consists of ten soldiers, and three sections make a platoon. They were asked to segregate their suitcases and trunks as per their sections, which were then left under a tree while they trooped into the barbershop area. It was quite a sight. Ten chairs were placed side by side in a row, with their craftsmen beside them, awaiting the new recruits. While one section at a time got their hair cut, those waiting filled out forms with personal information, including the next of kin to be informed in case of death or disability. When Chunni wrote his father's name, he thought of his mother, always kind and loving. How would she react if something happened to him?

After the haircut, they all stared at each other in wonder. They could not recognize each other without their long hair. 'Chunni,' shouted an unknown man. Chunni was the only recognizable one because he was so excited at the prospect of becoming a soldier that he had got a fauji haircut before coming to Srinagar. 'Suresh!' exclaimed Chunni to the unfamiliar face. 'You are looking so different.'

'Come, let us look for Narad,' said Suresh.

'Welcome to the army,' thought Chunni to himself with a smile. Inwardly, he was happy to become one of 'them'.

That afternoon they were all led to the Quarter Master Store, where they were issued uniforms, drill boots and other accoutrements to be worn by recruits. The uniforms were not well-fitting, but Chunni did not mind. He felt the pride of a soldier overwhelm him and vowed to become a good soldier and serve the country well.

The next morning, they had to wake up early and get ready before the sun was up. Chunni was eager, but he had to wake Suresh up. 'Wake up, lazy soldier. You don't want to be late on your first day as a soldier.' Besides, he was also excited because the opening address was to be given by the Commandant. He was excited at the thought of seeing a senior officer of the Army for the first time.

Brigadier A.S. Bains was a smart Sikh officer with a heavy-set beard. 'Welcome, boys, to the Indian Army and to the Jammu and Kashmir Light Infantry Regiment,' he said. 'You are fortunate to be selected for the army. It is a matter of pride to be an Indian soldier, as soldiering is the most respected profession. The JAKLI is a unique regiment, as this is the only regiment that was born in battle and purified in blood. When Pakistan invaded J&K in 1947, several volunteer groups offered resistance in different places in the state. These were truly motivated bands of people who fought the enemy with their own weapons.

'These groups were later reorganized as the Jammu and Kashmir Militia, a paramilitary force. This force has participated in all operations—1962, 1965 and 1971—and performed well in all operations. Therefore, in 1972, it was made into a regular regiment of the Indian Army. In 1976, our name was changed to JAKLI. A very strong foundation was laid by the original volunteers, and subsequent generations of soldiers have carried forward the ethos and spirit. It is your honour to join such a spirited organization.

'Another distinctive feature of our regiment is that we are sons of the soil. We have soldiers only from our state, J&K, and we have a mix of Hindus, Muslims and Sikhs. We also have the MMG—not the medium machine gun but mandir, masjid and gurudwara, all under one roof. All of us pray together and participate in each other's rituals. Halal and jhatka meat are cooked separately in each cookhouse. In short, it is just like the way you all live in amity in your villages.

'You are lucky to join this regiment, but we have to make you trained soldiers in less than one year. You will have a tough schedule. Lieutenant Colonel (Lt Col) Jai Narain here is your Training Battalion Commander.' Chunni recognized the officer—he had led the recruitment team in Doda. He had a very kind face.

The Commandant continued, 'Colonel Jai Narain and his team of instructors will turn you into good soldiers in the next year. But you will have to work hard. Remember, the more you sweat in peace, the less you will bleed in war. Good luck. May Allah Ta'ala, Durga Mata and Waheguru protect you and bless you all. Jai Hind.'

Chunni suddenly felt overwhelmed. It was a moving address. He felt goosebumps. He pledged to be a brave son of the soil and serve Bharat Mata to the last drop of his blood. He was prepared to undergo the toughest of training. In fact, he was raring to go.

The very next morning, when they started with the physical training (PT), Chunni realized it was much tougher than it looked. There were several short and not-so-short sprints, chin-ups, push-ups, abdominal exercises, rope climbing and more. Many recruits stopped running after some time, lagging behind in everything. Chunni was in high spirits and was among the first few recruits in all activities. Despite the tough routine, he was enjoying himself. They all heaved a sigh of relief when the hour of PT ended and they were given forty-five minutes to bathe, change into uniform and finish breakfast.

As they were leaving the PT grounds, Hav. Mohammad Sher Khan and his big moustache, from the first day was standing outside. 'I want you to fall in outside your barrack for the drill period after half an hour.' That practically reduced the breakfast break to thirty minutes. To fall in means to stand neatly in columns of three, they had learnt that morning from the PT Ustad (Instructor).

Drill Practice

Chunni, among the first to hit the showers, which were plentiful and laid out in a row, was also among the first to reach the cookhouse for breakfast. Breakfast was poori-aloo, which had never tasted so delicious. His first breakfast in a soldier's uniform. He felt pride sweep through him.

'C'mon, hurry up, or you'll be late,' boomed the voice of Hav. Sher Khan. Chunni turned and saw him standing at the door. He hurriedly ate the remaining pooris and gulped down his tea. As he hastened outside, he realized that he had seen Suresh eating his breakfast a few minutes after him, but he could not spot Narad. Then he realized that there were a few colleagues who had not been able to make it to breakfast.

'C'mon, c'mon, fall in, you lazybones. And they are asking us to make soldiers out of you,' barked Sher Khan again.

Outside the barrack, which was not far, Chunni was surprised to see that a few colleagues had already gathered to fall in. They were the unlucky ones who couldn't get ready in time for breakfast. They had all learnt a valuable lesson at the cost of missing poori-aloo.

Sher Khan made them stand in one line as per height. Chunni was towards the short end. Then he made them count. '*Ek-do mein ginti kar!*' he bawled out. They had to count '*ek-do, ek-do*' (one-two, one-two) alternately. Then with the help of two more HIs (also known as Drill Ustads), he taught them all how to make columns of two by separating those who counted 'ek' from those who counted 'do'.

'*Number ek, ek kadam aage; number do, ek kadam pichhe,*' Sher Khan commanded. Those who counted 'ek' moved a step ahead, and those who counted 'do' took a step back.

Then they were taught how to convert the columns of two into columns of three. Having made them stand height-wise first, the ten columns of three formed in a manner such that the tall soldiers were on either side and the shorter ones were towards the centre. Chunni was in the centre, facing Sher Khan's stare squarely. He held his gaze steadily.

Sher Khan gave a demonstration by calling the two other instructors to stand at attention and asked everyone to check their soldierly posture.

The three Drill Ustads then made them stand at attention and went around correcting their posture. 'Chest out, stomach in, chin up, heels together, toes pointing outwards, hands to the sides, fists clenched.'

Havildar Sher Khan explained, 'When I say "*Tez chal*," you must march with your left foot first. That's the way you march and swing the opposite arm in front. Left, Right, Left ... Left, Right, Left—'

They were all greenhorns and made many mistakes, but the Drill Ustads were patient with them on the first day. The second day, they were more demanding, and from the third day onwards, small punishments were meted out, like jumping up and down ten times with feet joined together or running till the Drill Square gate and back.

The Parade ground is called Drill Square and what we usually refer to as 'parade' is called drill. In fact, every organized activity is called 'Parade' in the army. Roll-call Parade is the fall-in in the evening, where the Platoon Havildar reads out orders and instructions for the day. There is Weapons Cleaning Parade; even going for prayers to Mandir Masjid Gurudwara on Sundays is called 'MMG parade'.

In those days, there used to be a Letter Writing Parade too, when all the soldiers sat down to write a letter home (but that was in the days before mobile connectivity).

The three Drill Ustads taught the recruits smart marching movements on the Drill Square, turning right, left and about-turns while marching as well as while standing.

While marching, they insisted the recruits march at a speed of 140 steps per minute. Chunni wondered how it mattered if they marched exactly the same number of steps each minute. But the Drill Ustads were so committed and used to slog even more than the recruits. One day, Chunni saw Sher Khan wiping his brow after removing his beret just after the Parade was over, despite the chill of the approaching winter.

To assuage his curiosity, during a casual moment with the Ustads, Chunni asked Sher Khan, 'Sir, why do we march at the speed of 140 steps per minute?'

'That's a good question,' Sher Khan replied. 'During the next class, I will talk about it, and a few other factors about drill.'

The next day, Chunni was eager with anticipation, but Sher Khan and his colleagues just continued with the gruelling routine of Parade and drill movements. Chunni felt disappointed. They had been divided into three groups of ten each, and each of the three instructors taught drill to ten of them, giving more personalized attention. It was also more tiring.

Ten minutes before the drill period was over, Sher Khan's command boomed across the Drill Square, 'Platooooon, *yahan pe Faaall-in*.' All three sections stopped their practice and rushed to the centre. Sher Singh ordered 'Savdhaan' and 'Vishram' once and then asked them to stand at ease, 'Araam-se'. This command is given to give a breather to the parade. He continued, 'You all have learnt the basics of Army Parade and drill over the last one week. However, you have much more to learn and practise. By the end of your training, I want you to be equal to us, if not better, in drill.'

'Will that ever be possible?' thought Chunni.

Sher Khan continued, 'Let me tell you some basics about drill. A soldier needs to practise drill for synchronized motions, which will bring more synergy to combat situations. Drill also improves a soldier's posture and gives you all a soldier's bearing. Have you ever wondered why you can recognize a soldier even when he is in civilian clothes in a market? You can make out a soldier because of his soldierly bearing, the way he carries himself. And that comes from drill. Parade practice also drills into all soldiers the basic quality of unquestioning obedience, which is so important for soldiers when in combat situations. And another thing, one of you asked me about marching speed, who was it?'

Chunni Lal raised his hand.

'What's your name?' Sher Khan asked.

'Chunni Lal, Sir.'

'Are you a sweeper? Are you a washerman?'

'No, Sir.'

'Then what are you?'

'I am a recruit, Sir.'

'Then say so. Let this be a lesson to all of you: in the Army, you have a rank and you must always prefix your rank before your name. So let's try again; what's your name?'

'Recruit Chunni Lal, Sir.'

Sher Khan appeared pleased that everyone had understood this important lesson. He continued, 'Your question was why we march at the speed of 140 steps per minute. The whole Indian Army marches at a speed of 120 steps per minute. Anything less than that looks sloppy. But JAKLI is light infantry. Light infantry and rifle regiments are traditionally lightly equipped and are the first to be deployed in battle. Hence, we march at a faster speed than the other regiments.'

'Thank you, Sir,' said Chunni. They had all learnt something interesting, he thought.

A Life Lesson on the Obstacle Course

One day, during the PT parade, they were taken to the obstacle course, and the Drill Ustad said, 'In the battlefield, you all may have to negotiate different kinds of obstacles. This obstacle course will prepare you for them.'

There was a ten-foot-long zigzag beam, about six inches wide. It began at a height of one foot above the ground and the height kept increasing to about 3 feet. Recruits had to stay balanced while running over it. Then they had to jump over a nine-foot ditch, climb over a six-foot wall, crawl under a two-foot-high wire mesh, vault over a high beam and more.

The first day, they learnt how to negotiate each obstacle one by one. The next day, they were asked to run over the ten-foot beam and clear all the other obstacles. This required strength, agility and stamina in equal measure, and Chunni found himself good at it. He was always in the lead. On the third day, they were divided into three sections of ten each. All three sections would start at the same time and were tasked with crossing all the obstacles at the earliest. Suresh and Chunni were in the same section, but Narad was in a different section.

Chunni was much faster than Suresh at crossing obstacles; in fact, he came first in his section. He beamed with pride at the Ustad. But the Ustad deflated him by saying, 'It's no good coming ahead of others. Look back at your section mates; some of them are struggling and some are helping each other. If you reach the objective ahead of the others, will you fight the enemy alone?'

Disappointed as he was, Chunni had learnt a valuable lesson, that of team spirit and camaraderie. In the army, more than anywhere else, a chain is as strong as its weakest link. In the army, it is a matter of life and death. This lesson stayed with Chunni Lal for life. He was determined to always give a helping hand to his comrades who were not as strong or as fast—in short, anyone who needed help.

Weapons Training and Firing

Another interesting and very important part of training was weapons training and firing. All the recruits were allotted a rifle each, and they had to draw the rifle from the Kote—an armoury where weapons were stored. They were to use it for weapons training and firing, then clean the weapon and its barrel and then deposit it back after it was inspected by the Armourer. An Armourer is a Specialist Havildar who inspects and repairs weapons.

For several days, they learnt how to strip and open the weapon and clean it. They learnt the names and functions of different parts and how to assemble the weapon. Chunni found it very interesting. 'You all will be able to strip and assemble a rifle blindfolded after a few weeks of practice,' their instructor announced.

'Why do we have to practise it blindfolded?' asked Chunni.

'That's a good question. Sometimes you may have to strip open your rifle to repair a stoppage in the dark,' the instructor replied. 'In such situations, your lives depend on it.'

At night, when it would get too cold, friends would sleep in twos so that they could wrap two blankets around themselves. 'When will we get to fire a rifle?' Chunni asked Suresh one night. 'I have joined to become a soldier, not a footballer or a boxer. And you can't become a soldier without firing weapons.' Football and boxing were two sports they enthusiastically and frequently participated in.

Chunni's wish was fulfilled the very next week, when two full days were scheduled for firing practice at the firing range. On these two days, there were no other classes. Targets in the shape of a man were affixed to the ground in front of a high wall. Between the targets and the high wall was a lot of mud piled up. This was to absorb the bullets. The recruits were taken to the firing point, which was at a distance of 25 metres (m) from the target.

They had to learn many drills and procedures, first without ammunition. 'Firing practice is also a risky business,' the Weapons Instructor explained. 'You should never, ever point a weapon at someone, even if it is empty. And even if you have to press the trigger of an empty weapon, you must still point it towards the targets or the sky before pressing the trigger. These are called safety precautions.'

Chunni found practical weapons training on the firing range very absorbing.

Initially, they learnt to fire their rifles from a lying position. Later they were given practice in firing from standing and kneeling positions. But firing from a battle-crouch position reflexively, without aiming, was what interested Chunni the most. Chunni was above average at firing but was very good in the battle-crouch position. He felt as if he was going to war soon.

On the firing range, there were several boards with inspiring slogans. The one that Chunni was most impressed by was '*Ek goli, ek dushman*' (one bullet, one enemy). Another good one was simply 'Shoot to kill'.

'What else,' thought Chunni. But he was to understand the profound meaning of the slogan soon. Hidden in it was the implication 'Kill or be killed.'

One day during firing practice, the Commandant, Brig. A.S. Bains, came to see their performance. Chunni was in the firing detail when he arrived. A firing detail consists of eight firers. After finishing their firing, all eight had to run and fetch their targets to show the results to the Commandant. They stood in a line holding their targets while he went around looking at them. The target is in the shape of a standing man. If a bullet hits the head or heart, the firer gets full marks. A bit on the side or the arms fetches fewer marks. But Brig. Bains had an interesting take on it. He said to the recruit standing beside Chunni, 'Your bullets have only hit the sides. Now the enemy is wounded, and wounded enemy soldiers are always more dangerous. So you must always shoot to kill. *Ek goli, ek dushman.*' 'Valuable lesson,' thought Chunni.

At the end of a day of firing practice, they had to return and clean their weapons. After that, the weapons had to be oiled and inspected by the Armourer before the soldiers could deposit them in the Kote. Some recruits had to repeatedly clean the barrel until it was passed by the Armourer.

Fieldcraft

Another very interesting subject in training to be a soldier was field craft. The recruits were taught the art of moving tactically in different situations, in different terrain conditions and in different formations, depending upon the operation of war they were practising. They were also taught the art of camouflage using watercolours on their face and hands. They also used leaves and rags on their equipment to visually break its shape.

Chunni was fascinated. They were shown a demonstration where they were asked to identify ten well-camouflaged soldiers hiding just around 20 m to 40 m ahead of them in the open ground. No one could point out more than four, so effective was the camouflage and their motionless posture. Another lesson learnt was that lying motionless helps you blend in with the ground.

Every day they would learn new things. It was extremely tiring but also very interesting. Chunni found himself looking forward to the next day's rigours every night as he fell asleep. The training sessions were not sequential, as narrated above. Every day brought a mix of subjects.

The day usually started with one hour of PT, at the end of which the recruits were drenched in sweat despite Kashmir's winter chill. They were given forty-five minutes to run to their barracks, bathe, change, gulp down breakfast (usually poori-aloo) and reach the next class, which was usually drill or Parade practice. One or two periods of drill were followed by weapons training, or field craft, or other subjects until lunchtime. Chunni's stomach would start rumbling towards the last class.

The recruits ran in squads of two to the langar, as the cookhouse was called, for lunch. En route, they would queue up at the Kote to deposit their rifles and other weapons. After lunch, they got an hour or more of well-deserved rest. Chunni and Suresh would hit the sack till woken up by some gruff voices announcing tea. Tea was brought to the barracks by the recruits in rotation. Chunni relished the extra-sweetened fauji tea in his enamel mug. My God, how much tea he had started consuming! His mother would have been aghast. But the winter chill of Srinagar, the fatigue of training, which required a pick-me-up cuppa and the *chai-pe-charcha* with newfound friends made them all very fond of tea. They made many friends within a matter of days. It seemed as if they had known each other for a long time. Whenever men face hardships together or share risks, the bond of friendship born out of such associations is always stronger. That is why it appeared to Chunni as though he had known his batchmates for years.

Games Parade

After tea, they would change into sports gear and fall in for games parade. The recruits had to play games—there was no choice in the matter. They were allowed to choose between football, hockey and volleyball in the main. However, all of them were encouraged to play all these games in turn. Chunni was more fond of football, and was good at it too. It was announced that each company[2] would field a company team and inter-company matches would be held after one month. Chunni was selected for the company football team and Suresh was in the reserve.

And there was boxing. Everyone had to participate in 'novices boxing'. Boxing is one sport that develops the qualities of aggressiveness, decisiveness, agility and a fighting spirit all at once.

The Games Parade was set for one hour but got stretched more often than not. The boys loved it. The fervour, or 'josh', and enthusiasm during a game of football had to be seen to be believed. Even sporting skills took a back seat to the josh. During inter-company matches, the josh of the spectators cheering for their own company was even more than that of the players.

Chunni was a valuable player for his company as a midfielder, but despite their best efforts, they lost the first match. The Company Havildar Major (CHM) gave them all a dressing down. He used such harsh words that it made Chunni wonder. After all, it was a game and one team had to lose. They tried their best. And what about sportsmanship?

The next day, they had a battalion roll-call. Roll-call parade was held every evening before dinner. All the recruits would dress in their muftis (a standard civilian outfit: a sky-blue shirt and light grey trousers) and assemble to receive orders and instructions. The CHM would take a headcount first, then issue orders. And then he would pass along special orders and instructions from the Training Battalion Commander or the Commandant.

But today was a special day. The Training Battalion Commander was coming for the roll-call to speak to them personally. He was Lt

Col Jai Narain, the same officer who had led the recruitment rally in Doda, where Chunni and Suresh had been selected together. He sounded very kind. He asked them if they were experiencing any difficulties, any problems. Chunni may have imagined it, but he thought that the CHM and other Havildars standing by the side were giving severe looks to the recruits, daring them to mention any problems.

'No, Sir,' the recruits shouted in unison.

'You may find the routine a little gruelling, but you will get used to it over time,' he said. 'You may not believe it when I say that this hard routine is for your own good. The more you sweat in peace, the less you will bleed in war. There are important lessons to be learnt each day. Yesterday, when one company lost the football match, you must have felt that the criticism was too harsh. Why is winning so important to us? Let me explain this to you. In our profession, there are no runners-up. Those who do not win often end up dead. In that split second, either you kill the enemy or he kills you. There are no silver medals. Every training activity here is to make you good soldiers who can take care of themselves. Only then will you be able to protect your motherland.' This put Chunni's mind at rest, as it had been bothering him why such a big deal was being made of losing a football match. With this, he learnt another valuable lesson that would come in very handy for him several times in combat situations.

'Games and sports also teach you team spirit and camaraderie,' the Lt Col continued. 'You can rest assured that your teammates or your soldier colleagues will not let you down. You will get their support during battle, even if they have to risk their lives for it. The same will be expected from you also. You will realize this in combat situations—that you can be surer of your section mates than even your family.'

Chunni was very impressed by what he had said and his manner of speaking, which was fatherly.

The training period had its ups and downs; some days were tougher than others. Then there were route marches and night marches that were to be completed while carrying full battle loads. Chunni was a stout lad and ever willing to help others. He was always carrying one extra pack during these marches to help some weaker boys. This lesson had been well learnt during the obstacle course training at the beginning of the year.

Gradually, Chunni could feel a change come over himself and even in the others. Hard physical training, route marches and a balanced diet were toning their muscles well. Those who had baby fat were losing it. They had to shave every day. From boys they had turned into men, raring to have a go at the enemy and at life.

Initially, they all used to get tired very quickly. Soon their stamina and endurance increased. At first, they used to fight the lack of sleep all the time. Gradually, they learnt to manage with less sleep. Earlier, all of them used to be fatigued all the time. Now they were full of josh most of the time.

Allotted a Battalion

At last, the day that they had been waiting for arrived. Two weeks before they completed their training, they were allotted the battalion that they would join. Not only would they join their battalion, but they would also spend the better part of their lives in these units, endearingly called the 'paltan'. Over the next couple of decades, if not more, they would spend more time in their paltans than at home with their families. They would live and die (some literally so) with their soldier buddies in the paltans. As seen above, the words battalion, unit and paltan are used interchangeably.

Chunni Lal was overjoyed that he and Suresh were going to the same battalion—the 8th Battalion, Jammu and Kashmir Light Infantry, 8 JAKLI for short. Even Narad was allotted to 8 JAKLI. They were all very happy. But their happiness was short-lived. A Subedar from another unit told them that all those going to 8 JAKLI were in for a hard time and tough luck because 8 JAKLI was training at the High Altitude Warfare School, preparatory to being deployed at the Siachen Glacier, the highest battlefield in the world.[3,4] The living conditions there were the toughest, with temperatures to the tune of minus 30 degrees Celsius even in summer (and far lower in the winter); the terrain was even harsher.[5]

Some of the boys felt demoralized by the news, but Lt Col Jai Narain, who had previously been the CO of the battalion, gathered all nineteen recruits posted to 8 JAKLI and addressed them. 'You all have been allotted one of the finest units in the Indian Army,' he said. 'I have had the proud privilege of commanding this battalion. It was raised as a volunteer force in Poonch in 1947. The Pakistan Army had laid siege to Poonch in November 1947 by occupying the mountain heights around the town. Several volunteers came forward and constructed a small airfield on the banks of the Poonch River. When the construction work was completed, the Indian Air Force could land aircraft with supplies, ammunition and troops to sustain the garrison. The volunteers then formed an outfit called the Border Scouts, who resisted the enemy. Many such volunteer groups had sprung up all over the (then) state of Jammu and Kashmir. Later, they were all reorganized as a paramilitary force called the Jammu and Kashmir (J&K) Militia.

'The Border Scouts were rechristened 8 J&K Militia. Born in battle and purified in blood, this brave battalion proved its valour in battle immediately on raising in the Poonch operations and won several gallantry awards, including one Vir Chakra. In 1971, the paltan was awarded two battle honours, besides many gallantry medals. Colonel Virendra Kumar, VrC, a hero of this operation, was the CO till recently. He is present at this regimental centre and will speak to you all tomorrow.'

The next day, Col Virendra Kumar came accompanied by Subedar Major (Sub. Maj.) Bhikam Singh. Both were not very tall, around the same height and each had a handlebar moustache. 'Welcome to 8 JAKLI, one of the bravest battalions,' said the Colonel. 'Col Jai Narain has already told you how our paltan was raised in battle. In the Army, we endearingly call our battalion paltan and the Jawans the boys.'

He continued, 'After displaying a superlative performance in Poonch on raising, in the 1971 Indo-Pak War, the 8th Battalion of Jammu and Kashmir Light Infantry [8 JAKLI] was the only unit that held on to its defences in the area of Chhamb when others fell back. We were awarded two battle honours—of Laleali and Picquet 707—in addition to several gallantry medals.'

Sub. Maj. Bhikam Singh interrupted, 'Col Saab was a Company Commander then at Laleali. In fact, he was the hero of Laleali who killed the attacking Pakistan Company Commander in hand-to-hand battle and was awarded the Vir Chakra. He was the CO of the paltan till recently.'

Chunni and Suresh looked at each other. Chunni was very impressed. They all felt motivated to join such an illustrious unit. Colonel Virendra then narrated something very interesting: 'After our impressive victory in the 1971 war, our new CO, Col S.C. Katoch (currently Brigadier) composed an inspirational song, which has become the unit song and is sung at unit functions as a motivational song. *Door hato ae duniya walo; Bharat desh hamara haihai* (Step aside, world; India belongs to us) ...'

Colonel Virendra closed by saying, 'I want to recite one stanza for you that is very relevant to you all today. This is talking about the four Vir Chakras that the battalion won in 1948 and 1971 put together:

> *Vir to hum me char hue,*
> *Ab Param ka chakkar pana hai.*
> *Agla mauka milne par,*
> *Seene pe ise lagana hai.*
> *(Four of our soldiers have so far been awarded the Vir Chakra,*
> *Now we have to attain the Param Vir Chakra.*
> *On the next possible opportunity,*
> *We have to pin it to our chest.)*

'SM Saab was telling me that some of you felt demoralized that you are going to join the paltan as it prepares to go into action at the Siachen Glacier. Look at it like this: you'll be able to tell veterans in your villages that what they could not see in fifteen years, you have seen in two years. I am confident that during this tenure, the paltan will make Brig. Katoch's words come true and get us all a Param ka Chakkar, or Param Vir Chakra, the highest gallantry award in India. You are the future of our paltan, and I am sure you will do us all proud. God bless.'

Chunni felt so moved. He could not wait to be launched into action. He looked longingly at the dark blue and yellow ribbon of the Vir Chakra on Col Virendra's chest and hoped that someday he would also win a Vir Chakra or a Param Vir Chakra.

After Col Virendra left, the SM Saab said jokingly, 'Khrew, where our battalion is located, is so close that if you wear your backpack and start walking tonight, before tomorrow morning, you'll be in the paltan.'

That evening, there was a Barakhana with all the recruits and instructors. The Commandant, Brig. Bains, also came for a short while. Basically, it was a celebration of the successful completion of their training period. Over drinks and dinner, they said goodbye to each other as well as to their instructors, thanking them for turning them into men from boys.

Gradually, Chunni could feel a change come over himself and even in the others. Hard physical training, route marches and a balanced diet were toning their muscles well. Those who had baby fat were losing it. They had to shave every day. From boys they had turned into men, raring to have a go at the enemy and at life.

3
'I Am a Soldier'

ALL THE RECRUITS were allotted different battalions located in different parts of the country. Chunni's unit was the closest, located in Khrew, near the JAKLI Training Centre. The next morning, an Army truck arrived to fetch all nineteen recruits assigned to 8 JAKLI. Chunni, Suresh and Narad were part of the group. It was a happy coincidence that all three of them had been recruited together and were now been allotted the same battalion.

Chunni was particularly pleased that Suresh was with him. They were buddies. As per the Indian Army's buddy system, all soldiers are assigned a buddy. When two soldiers are nominated as buddies, they live and operate together. They help and support each other on the battlefield and off it, tactically as well as logistically. A soldier's buddy knows him best. This system is a great reassuring factor for the soldiers themselves as well as for the army. Over time, the buddy becomes exactly as he is known, the best buddy for life. The equivalent of the present generation's BFF—best friends forever.

When they reached their battalion, 8 JAKLI, they were allotted companies. There are four fighting companies in a battalion and two more companies that offer fire support and logistic support, respectively. Chunni and Suresh were in the same company, Bravo Company. They remained buddies in the battalion too. Two other soldiers were also allotted Bravo Company. Narad was posted to Alpha Company. After spending a couple of days completing documentation and other formalities, they were taken to Sonamarg, where the battalion was undergoing training in preparation for its tenure at the Siachen Glacier, or simply 'the Glacier'.

The next day, they were addressed by their Company Commander, Major (Maj.) Varinder Singh, a very tall, burly Sikh officer with a deep voice. He had the physique of a Greek god and he twirled his moustache sometimes. It gave him a very soldierly demeanour. 'Welcome to one of the finest paltans of the Indian Army,' said Maj. Varinder. 'This battalion has a glorious history, and you are fortunate that you are directly being launched into operations. But first, you have to be trained for that. Your training for the last one year has made basic soldiers out of you, capable of operating in any terrain. Here we are training to prepare ourselves especially for mountain warfare and glacial conditions, because next year, we will be deployed in the higher reaches. Terrain and weather are as dangerous as the enemy itself, sometimes more because you don't encounter the enemy every day, but you have to negotiate the terrain and weather every day. There are snowstorms, blizzards, crevasses, avalanches and more. Take your training seriously. Your life depends on it.'

'Sir, why is fighting going on at the Siachen Glacier?' asked a Jawan sitting near Chunni.

'That is a good question,' said Maj. Varinder, affectionately called 'Viru' by his seniors and fellow officers in 8 JAKLI. He explained,

'Siachen Glacier has been a bone of contention between India and Pakistan for many years. The ceasefire line, and later the LoC, between the two countries has been demarcated up to a map point called NJ 9842. Thereafter, due to the inaccessibility of the area, it was agreed that the line would run northwards. Later, Pakistan started sponsoring foreign mountaineering expeditions into this area in order to establish its claim over the area. In the early 1980s, Pakistan tried to occupy the dominating mountain peaks in this area. As per the watershed principle that governs the LoC, the Siachen Glacier is in our territory. Hence, the Indian Army occupied the dominating heights ahead of the glacier to safeguard our territory.

'The LoC at the Siachen Glacier is called the Actual Ground Position Line, or the AGPL. The strategic importance of this area must also be remembered. The Glacier is not very far from the tri-junction of India, China and Pakistan. That is the reason why despite the vagaries of existence, it is imperative to guard it. And to be able to do that effectively, we must prepare ourselves in all respects to be able to operate at the Glacier.'

Their battalion was being trained as part of the Himalayan Brigade to be able to undertake operations in the glacial areas. For the next few months, they followed a gruelling training schedule. They learnt the use of ropes for rock climbing, slithering, rappelling and side rappelling. These complicated exercises would become a matter of routine while moving from one place to another on the Glacier. Chunni was also fascinated when they were taught different types of knots and how to use ropes adroitly. He was particularly impressed by two instructors, Nb Sub. Hem Raj and Hav. Mulk Raj. Both had been trained at the High Altitude Warfare School in Gulmarg.

During training for crossing difficult terrain that had steep falls and ice crevasses, Chunni and his fellow soldiers were taught how to move groups of five to seven men roped up—tying one rope around these men at intervals of a few feet so that if one man slipped and fell off a cliff, the others would be able to arrest his fall and assist him. Chunni recalled the invaluable lesson of the battle obstacle course in Srinagar, where he had learnt that reaching ahead of others was not as important as reaching together, securely. The soldiers were also taught all the precautions for weather, extreme cold and hygiene to be observed in the higher reaches.

In advanced training, they were put through snow training and ski training. While on night duty on the snow-covered mountains, Chunni mused that in the movies, snow-covered mountains looked very scenic and made for a romantic background setting, but bearing the chill while executing military manoeuvres was another thing altogether and not so pleasant. Yet he did not find himself cursing, as some others did. They were also taught how snow clearance was to be done from the tents every morning so that the tents could survive another day. Sometimes, they woke up with the tent half-covered with snow. Someone had to clear the snow from outside to let out the trapped soldiers. This happened often in the snow season. It speaks volumes about the trust soldiers have in each other and their camaraderie that they can sleep peacefully during heavy snowfall, knowing that their comrades will dig them out in the morning if needed.

That winter, Maj. Varinder Singh took his company for a training exercise. They had beaten a new path through fresh snow to a place called 'Ghumar Gali'. They had to beat the soft snow ahead of them with a spade to ensure they did not sink in it with their next step. They took seven days to reach their objective. Every morning, they would start early and walk from 0400 till 0800 hours (in the army, time is always measured using the twenty-four-hour clock).

They would have to beat the soft snow in many places before stepping into it, and yet they would sink nearly up to their thighs in many places. They would stop after 0800 hours each morning for fear of avalanches that were triggered when bright sunlight fell on loose snow. They ate pre-cooked meals that they had carried with them and brewed tea using melted snow on the paraffin stoves they carried. To Chunni, the tea tasted like hot nectar. He could feel the glow of its warmth travelling down his throat into his stomach. It felt like heaven. He had often heard that drinking tea drove sleep away, but Chunni found himself drifting off to sleep while the 'tea warmth' in his stomach lingered.

Early the next morning, at 0400 hours, the same routine would resume. Their progress was slow, but it tested their snow-craft and rock-climbing skills and taught them valuable lessons in ice-craft and survival, and, most of all, built the feeling of camaraderie, a sense of belonging to the company, the battalion and the Indian Army.

On the seventh day, they reached Ghumar Gali, tired and weary, short of breath due to the lack of oxygen. However, this had not dimmed the enthusiasm and josh in Chunni and the other soldiers. This was thanks to the strong spirit of camaraderie amongst the patrol members and, above all, the inspirational leadership of Maj. Varinder Singh. Chunni felt that he could easily risk his own life for his Company Commander or on his orders.

They were also at the end of their rations. 'Has anyone got any gur left?' asked Viru. *Gur*, or jaggery, is the soldier's favourite as it is sweet, keeps the body warm and is good for digestion. Only Chunni had a medium-sized piece left.

'Let us all celebrate by sharing it and return to our base. Well done, boys,' said Viru. When Chunni tried to hand it over to him, he smiled and said, 'You take the first bite and pass it down the line. I will have the last bite. His smile widened when he said, 'Make sure something is left for me.' Chunni took a small bite and passed it to Suresh, who did the same and passed it on to the next soldier. On and on it went till Maj. Varinder had the last bite. Chunni felt that this simple act of sharing a small piece of jaggery was a bonding ritual.

'*Bahadur Bravo ke kahadur Jawano,*' (Fearless Soldiers of the Bahadur Bravo) said the Major. 'Now we must start back on the track that we have taken the pains to create.' They retraced their steps to the base and made it by the same evening. All the companies were carrying out similar training activities. The whole battalion was preparing seriously to be launched in operations at the Glacier.

Chunni started to feel so much at home in Bahadur Company that it felt like family. But sometimes, especially while falling asleep, he would miss his family. He yearned to find comfort in the warmth of his mother's embrace. He also wanted to hug his father and brothers.

FROM ONE FAMILY TO ANOTHER

The next year, in the summer, Chunni and Suresh went on leave together. This was their first vacation as soldiers, and their parents felt so proud of them. Chunni also felt as if he had grown from a boy in to a man. Everyone at home and in the village treated him with newfound respect. His mother had tears of joy in her eyes often and would hug him, saying, 'I missed you so much, my son. Army life is risky, isn't it? Promise me you will take good care of yourself and not take unnecessary risks.'

His father spoke to him as one speaks to an adult. He repeatedly told him how proud he felt when other men in the village congratulated him deferentially for sending his son to the army. 'I will also be able to get a door installed in the cow barn with the money you brought in from your soldier's pay,' he told his son with a mixture of love and respect. On an impulse, Chunni hugged his father.

Chunni found himself quite pleased with this new status of his. He stood in front of the mirror and smiled to himself. He then saluted the mirror and said, 'Jai Hind'.

He liked being in his village. He enjoyed the breeze bowing through the tall trees. The sun-kissed mountains seemed so warm in comparison to the freezing snow-craft training in Sonamarg. The crisp mountain air in his lungs filled him with enthusiasm. He remained in high spirits, in a mood of dreamy goodwill towards all. He did not have many friends, but a few from his schooldays came by to hear of his fauji exploits. Despite the good time he was having in his village, towards the end of his month-long leave, he had started getting restive and wanted to get back to his unit. He had never realized he would miss his soldier colleagues so much. When he told his friends, they made fun of him. But secretly, he was pleased to realize that his heart longed to be with his band of brothers. There was another family he had become part of, the one with whom he would live and die, figuratively as well as literally.

He and Suresh coordinated to travel back together. During the journey, they exchanged stories about their friends and family. As they boarded the Army transit bus from Ramban, it felt like a homecoming. The all-too-familiar olive-green uniform, the crisp Army lingo and the smartly turned-out soldiers. They felt like they belonged, but Chunni tugged at his hair self-consciously. His hair had grown out of the Army crewcut.

During training for crossing difficult terrain that had steep falls and ice crevasses, Chunni and his fellow soldiers were taught how to move groups of five to seven men roped up—tying one rope around these men at intervals of a few feet so that if one man slipped and fell off a cliff, the others would be able to arrest his fall and assist him. Chunni recalled the invaluable lesson of the battle obstacle course in Srinagar, where he had learnt that reaching ahead of others was not as important as reaching together, securely.

4

Bravery on Top
Induction into the Siachen Glacier

Once Rfn[6] Chunni Lal returned to his unit after leave, there were more lectures on precautions to be observed in high altitude and glacial areas. Everything was in preparation for their extreme high-altitude glacier tenure. Viru told them to follow everything they learnt, as their lives would depend on it. He explained, 'High altitude area starts from 9,000 feet upwards. The human body has to get acclimatized to the shortage of oxygen in the air above that. Therefore, we will spend six days getting used to it by taking short walks and gradually increasing the distance every day.

'When we cross 12,000 feet, and later at 15,000 feet this drill will have to be repeated over four days each.[7] Otherwise, we will not be able to function at those heights. And we don't need to only function, we have to be combat-ready there.' He paused for effect and said, 'If we get an opportunity for combat, I'm sure Bahadur Bravo soldiers will be more than a match for the enemy.'

Little did he know that his words would be prophetic.

In August that year, the unit started inducting towards Partapur, staying there for a few months then staging forward to the Base Camp, located at the snout or the lowest tip of the Siachen Glacier. This was at an altitude of 12,000 feet and the place where the second stage acclimatization was carried out. While there, one day as Chunni returned to his barrack after completing his sentry duty at the Kote, Suresh told him in a heavy voice, 'Bad news, yaar. One of our unit vehicles has gone down in an avalanche and we lost nine out of the ten soldiers travelling in it. Only one survived.' A pall of gloom had descended on the paltan. These were such wasteful casualties and futile deaths, Chunni felt. Death in combat was more purposeful. But such are the occupational hazards of soldiering.

All units and soldiers inducting into the Glacier were trained at the Siachen Battle School at the Base Camp for couple of months in different skills required to survive and operate in the climate and conditions that lay ahead for them. They were taught, and they practised in advance, ice-craft skills like climbing ice walls with the help of specialized mountaineering equipment like ice axes and crampons. Chunni found it fascinating to fix crampons to his snow boots. These had spikes below and in front to secure a good grip on the snow while hanging on with one hand to an ice wall using an ice axe. They learnt to use crampons and ice axes till they could climb near vertical ice walls, even while carrying their rucksacks, which contained their battle loads (weighing around 15 to 20 kg) and personal weapons. One day during training, a short Junior Commissioned Officer (JCO) by the name of Nb Sub. Bana Singh was taking a class to brief the Jawans about hygiene precautions to be observed while living on the Glacier. Chunni was struck by the firm and steady tone of the JCO.

'If your socks get wet due to snow, you must change into dry socks as soon as possible, otherwise you're likely to develop chilblains or frostbite,' he warned them. 'The manifestations start with numbness and grow into an acute tingling sensation. A bad case of frostbite can even lead to amputation of toes.'

A Jawan sitting next to Chunni said, 'You better remember that these small things will make a big difference to our lives at the Glacier.' His name was Laxman Dass. By his accent he did not appear to be from Jammu. After the class Chunni learnt that Laxman Das hailed from his neighbouring district of Kishtwar. Chunni recalled his father telling him that people from Kishtwar were smart and slick talkers, they bordered the Kashmir region and could understand the Kashmiri language just like he could. Between Chunni, Suresh and Laxman, they had the areas of Bhaderwah, Doda and Kishtwar covered and they all understood the Kashmiri language.

Another very important facet they were trained in was the skill of walking through snow-covered rocks and cliffs. Chunni's Company Commander, Viru, briefed the soldiers of his company on what lay ahead for them.

'The terrain is full of treacherous slopes and there is always a danger of crevasses,' he said. 'A crevasse is formed when hard-packed ice sometimes cracks due to temperature variations. These cracks can be a few inches to several feet wide and can go up to hundreds of feet in depth. The temperature at the Glacier is in the region of minus 55 degrees during winter and minus 30 degrees during summer, but at the bottom of a crevasse, the temperatures are much lower. Hence, we all will rope-up while walking, which means five to seven men will be tied to a rope at intervals, so that if a soldier falls into a crevasse, the others can pull him out. If not rescued promptly, a man can freeze to death in the extremely low temperatures in the crevasse. In some of the known crevasses on the frequented routes, aluminium ladders have been placed permanently as bridges.'

He added, with morbid humour, 'However, if a soldier falls into a crevasse and he is not rescued promptly, his smile is frozen for eternity.' The human body remains preserved in that super-chilled temperature of a crevasse.

Viru went on to explain a connected facet. 'Nothing decays on the Glacier due to the extreme cold sub-zero temperatures. Whether it is trash or foodstuff, rotten vegetables or human excreta, everything surfaces afresh when the top layers of snow melt a bit in the summers. So, we have to be very careful about waste management.'[8]

Gearing Up and Being Deployed at a Post

All soldiers being inducted into the Glacier were issued special clothing and mountaineering equipment. The snow boots, socks and garters were all imported stuff that mountaineering expeditions use. The induction itself was a long, drawn-out process that took a couple of weeks. Chunni was a part of the induction party that went by foot, while some key personnel were taken by helicopters.

Time-consuming as it was, going on foot helped to acclimatize the soldiers as they gained altitude gradually, and their lungs and muscles kept getting used to the rarefied atmosphere step by step, literally. From Base Camp, it took four days to reach the Battalion Headquarters (HQ) at Kumar. Before and after the Battalion HQ, were a series of administrative camps for night halts.

Chunni was deployed on his platoon post. A post is a group of bunkers built on a high mountain peak so that they can dominate the area around by observation and fire of weapons. It is required to hold such positions to ensure that there is no enemy ingress, and to fire one's weapons in case the enemy tries to creep in. For this, a constant 24/7 vigil is needed. Chunni recalled how freezing cold it felt when he was on sentry duty for observation purposes, especially at night. It is easier to walk from one point to another than to stand on sentry duty, more so at posts where there is hardly any space to even pace around to keep oneself warm. If any soldier wondered why there was a need to maintain sentry duties round the clock, the Company Commander's briefing answered all such questions.

'Boys,' he said, 'we have to be extremely careful and never let down our guard while at the Glacier. While the terrain and climate are constant enemies, we must not lower our guard against the enemy. Just before our unit was inducted, the previous unit suffered two casualties, when one JCO and one NCO (Non-Commissioned Officer) died due to unprovoked firing by the enemy at Sonam Post.'

Chunni, Suresh and Laxman were together at their post and had struck up a good kinship. The rigours appeared too tough initially, but gradually they became used to it. Their bodies were also adapting to the extreme cold. This is the process of acclimatization.

In the army, information is disseminated on a need-to-know basis. Therefore, they only knew what was happening in their company. But one day, Chunni and Suresh heard a lot of firing in the distance, more than the usual exchange. That night, Chunni heard during dinner that there had been casualties at another post of their unit, perhaps even an officer had been hit. This was disturbing news. Soldiers feel such strong bonds of brotherhood that none of them could sleep well that night.

The next morning, the Company Commander visited their post and explained the situation to them, which was very grave. This is the standard operating procedure (SOP) in the army. Whenever an incident of great importance takes place, the troops are briefed about the details, nature and gravity of the incident on a need-to-know basis. This prevents the rise of wild rumours and provides authentic details of the incident down to the last man. This motivates the soldiers to respond accordingly.

Viru's tone was calm but laden with sadness. When he spoke, it was clear he was controlling his emotions. 'A very sad incident has taken place. You all can see the Northern shoulder of Bilafond La Pass from a distance. The enemy had occupied it last month and our side came to know of it when unprovoked firing opened on the Bihar Regiment unit that was here before us, where we lost one JCO and a Jawan.' Though referring to the personnel of another unit, Viru said 'we', because that is the sense of ownership soldiers feel for the whole army.

'Since long, this enemy post—called the Left Shoulder—has been interfering with troop movement and helicopter movement in the area, as it is the most dominant post in the area. Our posts, like Sonam and Amar, which are totally air-maintained posts, are facing the pinch because we are unable to replenish food, fuel and ammunition in time. This is creating hardships for them. How can we sit comfortably if our brothers are facing such difficulties? So, our CO, Col Arun Prakash Rai had sent a reconnaissance patrol to ascertain the enemy deployment, led by Lt[9] Rajiv Pandey; Nb Sub. Hem Raj Sharma was his Second-in-Command. There were seven more Jawans, including Hav. Mulk Raj.' Chunni clearly recalled Hem Raj and Mulk Raj as good instructors of mountain climbing and ice craft.

Viru was continuing, 'The patrol very bravely negotiated the 1,200 feet high ice-wall using ice axes and other mountain climbing equipment and managed to reach the Saddle[10] on the razor-sharp ridgeline.'

'When you look at the near 90-degree-slope, you wonder how our soldiers could climb the feature,' said Viru. 'Havildar Mulk Raj was such a good mountaineer. He and Nb Sub. Hem Raj used their ice axes to climb the ice wall. It was an incredible feat of bravery, mountaineering skills and confidence. Fortunately, there was no response from the enemy. Emboldened, they decided to exploit the situation tactically and started advancing towards the enemy post by crawling in the snow.

'Suddenly, enemy opened up with machine-gun fire at close range. We lost six Bravehearts including Lt Pandey and Nb Sub. Hem Raj. It is a sad incident, but it shows that in the Indian Army the leaders lead from the front. Suraj, who is a wrestler, actually tied a wounded casualty, Rfn Darshan on to his back and climbed down. Darshan was hit in his stomach by machine gun bullets, and Suraj first had to put his entrails inside and tie up his stomach. Such is the stuff our paltan's Bravehearts are made of.'

He paused for a moment or two to get his emotions under control and then continued, 'This brave patrol, which included mountaineers like Hem Raj and Mulk Raj, have painstakingly tied the rope and we swear on their dead bodies that we will avenge their deaths.'

'Where are their dead bodies, Sir?' asked Chunni.

'They lie where they had fallen', replied Viru, 'That is why it is all the more important that we attain our objective and get our soldier brothers back.'

He paused for them to take that in, and then asked in emphatic tones, 'Who all will volunteer to go for an attack on the Left Shoulder? Let's have a show of hands.'

'Me, Sir!' replied everyone in unison and everyone's hand went up promptly, without a single exception.

'Good! I expected nothing less from Bahadur Company,' replied Viru.

A Jawan sitting next to Chunni said, 'You better remember that these small things will make a big difference to our lives at the Glacier.' His name was Laxman Dass. By his accent he did not appear to be from Jammu.

5

Frozen and Skyward
The Highest Attack in the World

After the sad loss of 2Lt Rajiv Pandey and his boys, the whole battalion was incensed. There was grief, but there was more outrage. One thought was uppermost in everyone's mind—how to avenge the deaths of our fallen comrades? Someone had lost a *numbari* (a batchmate), someone had lost a *granhi* (a man from his village), some a relative and some a military buddy from their section.

Senior officers of the battalion spoke with each other about how to retrieve the bodies of those soldiers that lay close to Pakistan's post at the Left Shoulder. The higher leadership was acutely conscious of the fact that as long as the Left Shoulder remained in Pakistan's control, it would be difficult to maintain Indian posts by helicopters; there was no land route to walk to Sonam Post and other posts in that area. Moreover, the Left Shoulder Post dominated other posts by fire and observation. The enemy brought down effective artillery fire and fired their machine guns and other weapons, causing heavy casualties to Indian soldiers and damage to bunkers and materials, all of which were so hard to replace.

It was, therefore, decided to launch an attack and capture the Left Shoulder. The battalion, 8 JAKLI, readily volunteered to undertake the operation and began planning for the highest attack in the world. It was a herculean task. Nowhere in the world had an assault taken place at an altitude where men cannot even walk due to lack of oxygen in the rarefied air. Mountaineers carry oxygen cylinders to breathe, but these soldiers would carry battle-loads and weapons to shoot. For mountaineers, survival is at stake. They have to save themselves from the harsh terrain and the vagaries of the weather. These soldiers had to overcome the altitude, the terrain and the weather and then fight the enemy. Kill or be killed. No runners up.

Volunteers were asked to participate in the attack, and of these fortunately there was no dearth. It was decided that an assault base will be established at the base of the Left Shoulder Massif—upon which the enemy post was situated. The assault base is the place where the task force would build up and from where the attack would be launched. Most of area around the assault base was not under enemy observation. Nevertheless, the movement of soldiers with weapons, supplies etc., i.e. their 'build-up', to the assault base, and their training were major challenges.

For instance, three helicopter sorties were required to take two soldiers to the assault base, which was to function as the firm base for launching the attack at the Left Shoulder. Flying at such altitudes placed such severe load restrictions that one chopper could only take one soldier without his battle gear and one chopper would carry the battle load of two soldiers after they had been ferried. To add to it, weather played truant on several days. Hence the build-up of the task force was a painstakingly slow process.

Viru volunteered to lead the task force that would capture the Pakistan Quaid Post. What is a post? On the AGPL, just as on the

Line of Control (LoC), there is a requirement to guard the boundary between the two countries day and night. A post is a group of bunkers on top of a mountain peak that can dominate the area all around for considerable distance by observation and firing of weapons. A bunker is a small 8 feet by 10 feet, mostly dug underground. It has a reinforced roof as protection against enemy shelling or bombing. What would be ventilators of the room are the loopholes of the bunker, through which weapons can be fired, keeping the soldiers safe from enemy's firing.

Rfn Chunni Lal was at the Siala Post, which formed a shoulder of Sia La Pass. He along with Rfn Laxman Dass and Rfn Nek. Ram volunteered from Siala. So many volunteers were pouring in from other companies too. This, despite the fact that it was the riskiest mission, and despite the fact that India had lost the six Bravehearts who had attempted to get there.

What makes a soldier want to put himself in harm's way?

What makes a soldier do what he does, straight from the heart?

Is it the salary or pension? Is it the benefits and the perks? Is it for a few thousand rupees and no bonus that a soldier is willing to risk his life?

He does it for his comrades. He does not want to let down his colleagues. He would rather die than let down the good name and honour or 'izzat' of his battalion.

He risks his life for Naam, Namak, Nishan—the 'unit ki izzat' its honour is the Naam; the loyalty to the regiment is Namak; the flag of the regiment, its Nishaan; for the battle honours and awards that the paltan has won—and because he wants to exceed that.

We soldiers serve with the concept of unlimited liability. When a soldier goes into the battlefield, he is prepared to die for his country, for the mission, for his comrades. Yet we always have more volunteers than we need to participate in high-risk operations.

There were so many volunteers for this operation that they had to be screened. At the Battalion HQ at Kumar, the Adjutant, Captain (Capt.) Rajiv Maithani, would screen the boys and the CO, Col A.P. Rai, would then give a pep talk to the selected Siachen Senanis (warriors). Besides taking a cursory look at the soldiers for good health and high morale of the volunteers, those soldiers who hailed from the mountainous areas of Kishtwar, Doda and Bhaderwah were welcome as they were naturally more adept at operating in higher altitudes. A couple of soldiers from Ladakh were also included for this reason.

Those who were excluded were crestfallen. Salute the Indian soldier, who wants to put himself in harm's way; who is sad rather than relieved when excluded from a mission in which he has to risk his own life in face of the enemy, terrain and weather.

Commanding Officer Col A.P. Rai addressed the Siachen Senanis and told them of our proud history. 'Last month, the Pakistanis killed our Bravehearts of Rajiv Pandey Patrol. Not only do we have to avenge that, we also have to get their bodies back. If we don't get the bodies back, what reply will we give their families? If we don't finish their unfinished task, how can we live with ourselves? Their souls will rest easy only when we complete their unfinished mission of capturing the Left Shoulder. I am so proud that nearly everyone in my brave battalion has volunteered when we asked for volunteers. It is in true spirit of our origins as a volunteer force.

'Our battalion was raised as a volunteer force during operations in face of the enemy in 1947, and we won laurels and gallantry medals as a fledgling paramilitary force. We participated in many operations and won one Vir Chakra and five Mention-in-Despatches. In the 1971 Indo–Pak War, ours was the only battalion that repulsed repeated enemy attacks in Chamb in J&K and held on while others withdrew. Today that is the only launch-pad India has west of the Munawar Tawi River.

'Our paltan was awarded two battle honours—Laleali and Picquet 707—and a host of gallantry medals. Such were our forefathers. Don't we want live up to that tradition, get our bodies back, and pay homage to the Virgati Prapt (those who made the supreme sacrifice) by completing their unfinished mission of capturing the Pakistani post? It won't be easy, but that's what our paltan is all about. When the going gets tough, the tough get going. Are you all ready?'

The boys shouted back their willingness to fulfil the assigned task, even at the expense of their lives. That is the stuff Indian Army is made of. Unquestioning obedience, unlimited liability, no incentive, no bonus, yet willing to die for a cause.

A General Salute to the Indian soldier.

Building Up the Assault Task Force

The build-up began on 8 June 1987. Havildar Babu Ram of C Company was the first man to go and was flown-in on an Army Aviation Corps' Cheetah helicopter. Kumar, the Battalion HQ, was at 16,000 feet and the assault base at the base of the Left Shoulder was at around 20,000 feet. As a result, the chopper had severe load-carrying restrictions. It may appear funny, but as mentioned earlier, it required three sorties to ferry two soldiers across—two sorties to carry one soldier each without their battle-loads, and the third sortie to carry their loads and ammunition.

As mentioned above, the first to be flown in was Hav. Babu Ram, followed by Hav. Balwant Singh, a driver in the Mechanical

Transport Platoon who had volunteered to be a part of the assault task force. The third chopper ferried their personal loads, including ammunition. The third soldier to be inducted was Hav. Darshan Lal. Then the weather packed up and the choppers could not fly due to poor visibility, rather nil visibility. That was the end of the induction for the day.

So, it was not only the load-carrying restrictions that made the induction of a sixty-strong task force a tedious and a protracted process. The weather was. more often than not, a spoilsport as is wont to happen frequently in high-altitude areas. It was also against the regulations for the helicopters to fly after noon for their own safety, as the weather deteriorated rapidly post-noon without warning on most days.

All of this led to instances where the chopper would stay put for the night at the Sonam Post where it had landed. This caused its own problem dynamics—freezing oils and the chopper not being able to start the next morning. One could keep talking of the challenges that merely living on the Glacier imposed on the army, but let us get back to our induction of the task force near the post at the base, which was to serve as the launch pad for the attack on the enemy post at the Left Shoulder. This assault base was at an altitude of 20,000 feet.

Meanwhile, volunteers continued to reach the Battalion HQ daily, after having been put through a confirmatory medical check-up at the Base Camp under the keen supervision of Maj. R.K. Singh. It was important that the soldiers volunteering for this superhuman task of participating in the highest attack in the world be super-fit; we could not afford to have medical casualties in an operational scenario.

At the Battalion HQ they also went through the process of screening by the Adjutant and initial briefing and motivation by the

CO. Viru had volunteered to be the Task Force Commander. Captain Anil Sharma was his Second-in-Command, and Sub. Harnam Singh, Sub. Sansar Chand and Nb Sub. Bana Singh were the three assault section commanders. Fifty-seven Bravehearts were selected from among the volunteers.

For a couple of days the weather did not permit any flying. The first three soldiers had to stay by themselves. On their second day there, Pakistan soldiers threw something down at them. The Pakistan post was over a thousand feet higher. Our soldiers' first thoughts were that their presence had been detected, which is why the enemy had thrown down one of the bodies of 2Lt Rajiv Pandey's patrol. That would be sacrilegious.

Angered, they crawled forward to investigate, all the time fearing that the enemy would start firing at them as they were in the open without any cover. Their all-white extreme cold snow clothing helped them blend with the environment. They could not be observed easily. Yet, to a keen observer, movement could be spotted. It was a clear day.

Balwant and the other two were crawling slowly, breathing laboriously, the snow crunching beneath their weight, expecting the enemy to start firing at them any moment. They must have been in the open for twenty minutes, but it seemed like two hours. They reached the object safely, only to discover to their relief that it was a sleeping bag belonging to the enemy soldiers that seemed to have blown away with the wind. Loss of a sleeping bag at such sub-zero temperatures can be catastrophic. But their fears of defiling our soldier's body were put to rest. It also was an indication that their fears that they had been observed by the enemy seemed to be unfounded. And that was such a relief. Double relief was what they felt as they started their slow crawl backwards.

Over the next few days, the build-up at the assault base was slow, the task force commander and section commanders reached there so that they could get acclimatized, carry out reconnaissance, examine their options and make their attack plans, as well as contingency plans. Contingency plans are the plans in various situations when things go wrong, or if they don't go as per the plan. In the army, operations are planned meticulously with alternatives and backups. After all, lives are at stake, a good plan or bad makes the same difference as between life and death.

It was decided that the build-up of sixty persons by chopper would take an inordinately long time, especially due to the uncertainties imposed by the weather. The CO discussed the issue with Maj. Varinder Singh and Capt. Rajiv Maithani who were at Kumar, and decided to open a land route to the assault base, extremely tough though it promised to be. The CO dared not discuss the plan with the other senior officers of the battalion because the radio communication network, the only reliable means of communication with them, was prone to interception by the enemy. Surprise could be lost, and if the enemy knew of our attack plan in advance, the soldiers would suffer heavy casualties. Surprise is a principle of war that can fetch disproportionate dividends. Hence, it was imperative that surprise must be maintained at any cost.

Lt Col Inderjit Gupta was the second in command of the Battalion. He was a tall, well built man, who worked very hard at his good physique and was terribly fit. He was the right man to take up the challenge of opening the land route to the assault base. No one had ever walked to Sonam Post near it at the Siachen Glacier. Not only were the soldiers ferried to their posts by helicopters, but so were also their stores, supplies and other logistic requirements, including ammunition and military equipment.

Walking to the assault base would not be an easy feat, but Indian soldiers are hardy and determined, especially when they are well led and are truly motivated, as were the soldiers of this battalion. They were consumed by this mission to attack the enemy post at 21,000 feet and bring back our dead. Such determination on the back of a glorious war record gives wings to soldiers.

The land route was opened, and on 19 June 1987 the balance of the Jawans participating in the operation moved in a walking convoy towards the assault base. It was a dark-to-dark move, starting at 0500 hours while it was still dark, and reaching around fourteen hours later, after sunset at about 1900 hours. Rfn Chunni Lal walked along with his comrades from his Bravo Company—CHM Bharat Singh, Rfn Laxman Dass and Rfn Ravi Kumar. It was a slow march, as they all carried their personal loads, their weapons and ammunition totalling around 20 kg. In such higher reaches, walking through snow has its own difficulties. The pace is slow for two reasons. The snow boot sinks a bit into the snow with a crunch, if the snow is fresh and if not, then the path is slippery. Besides, the lack of oxygen in the air forces the soldiers to walk slowly, placing one foot in front of the other.

The soldiers halted at an artillery gun position at Echo DZ enroute for rest. The DZs are designated drop zones where helicopters dropped supplies for the soldiers. Chunni felt his legs ache far more than they had ever. Same was the case with every soldier. However, there was stronger emotion in all of them—the spirit of revenge. They were all consumed by the need to avenge the death of their brave brothers, who had made the supreme sacrifice as a part of Pandey Patrol, as it had come to be known.

During this long march, at couple of places, they saw a tall pillar of snow, with some tents or shelters on top. There was a pathway to come down with a couple of ladders also placed at some spots.

Chunni asked CHM Bharat Singh about it, saying, 'This seems odd, Sir.'

The CHM explained, 'This is called the pillaring effect. At these high altitudes, when temperatures rise somewhat in summers, the fresh snow melts a bit in areas that get good sunlight. However, in some pockets where tents are pitched or shelters are made, and the snow is also packed tight with steel channels for helicopters to land, the snow does not melt. After a couple of seasons, these pockets with tents and shelters and those with the helipads rise above the surroundings, presenting a surreal picture.'

Chunni could not get over his amazement.

The long and arduous march carrying personal loads took around fourteen hours as mentioned above, and a platoon strength of thirty personnel the assault base at 1900 hours. It was dark by then, so they could creep in unnoticed by the enemy. Such tactics meant the difference between life and death, and one had to be constantly conscious of what could go wrong. In order to survive, when so many things could go wrong at every step.

Over the next few days, the soldiers acclimatized, the commanders made their plans and briefed their men. They all maintained their weapons. In the Army the term 'maintained' includes cleaning and oiling of weapons to ensure that the weapon would fire smoothly and that there will be no stoppages. They were also test fired.

They lived in makeshift tents made of the parachutes that had been used to paradrop supplies. The walls were mostly made of the jerry cans in which kerosene had been dropped; in these jerry cans and later the empty ones were being put to good use. They made bivouacs if jerry cans were not available. In bivouacs, the parachutes were tucked in the snow. Chunni Lal lived in a bivouac along with Girdhari, Laxman, Ravi and CHM Bharat. One night, there was a heavy snowfall and next morning they found Girdhari had died of suffocation. He was sleeping next to the wall and snow pressed on the tent fabric on his side, because of which he could not breath. He died in his sleep.

This was the last straw. Earlier, a few Jawans had complained of minor problems like numbness in fingertips and toes. After Rfn Girdhari's death, Viru decided that it would be best to advance the attack. Who knows how many non-operational casualties they might suffer if they waited any longer? The attack had been planned for 30 June 1987, Viru discussed it with his team and took his CO's okay to launch it a week earlier, on 23 June.

The Attack

The task force was divided into four sections.

Capt. Anil Sharma headed the Cut off group. They were tasked to attack the enemy administrative base and cut off the only route that led to the Left Shoulder enemy post from their administrative base, in order to isolate the post. It was their job to ensure that no reinforcements could reach the post during the operation and no soldier from the post could get away from the post.

The other three sections were assault sections and were led by one of the three JCOs. They would attack the enemy post and clear it of enemy soldiers, bunker by bunker. While it involves close quarter battle, possibly including hand-to-hand combat, a very important component of an assault also involves occupying defences on the post in a viable manner that they can beat back an enemy counter-attack. The loopholes and firing emplacements are facing the wrong way for that. They have to be turned towards the enemy's rear positions from where a counter-attack is likely to materialize. This activity is known as 'turning the defences'.

Subedar Harnam's section was selected to lead the assault. Two veteran NCOs in this section were Hav. Darshan Lal and Hav. Babu Ram. Rifleman Chunni Lal was a dependable member of this section. Like the others, he too was full of josh and eager to attack.

Hunting for Pandey Patrol's Rope

In accordance with the modified plan, the attack was to begin on 23 June, full one week before the originally planned date. The force moved cautiously to the general area where rope had previously been fixed by Havildar Mulk Raj and his team (belonging to 2Lt Rajiv Pandey's patrol). Once this rope was found the men would use it to climb more than 1,000 feet up a sheer vertical ice wall to reach the Saddle. The plan was to climb up to the Saddle and use it as the firm base, and launch the attack on the Left Shoulder from there. A firm base is a secure place from where an attack is launched. Weapons are deployed on its sides to ensure its safety and security.

The soldiers of the leading section moved cautiously to the place where they would find the rope. Surprise was of essence. Walking in snow is always tricky. Due to fresh snowfall, Chunni felt himself sinking in the snow at every step. Moreover, walking was very laborious at 20,000 feet. At last, they reached the intended spot and began searching for the rope.

Chunni Lal and Laxman Das were in the forefront with their section. Chunni chipped away with his ice axe along with others, sometimes using gloved hands to push away loose snow. Try as hard as they may, all efforts were frustratingly in vain. They just could not find the rope. It had been buried under the snow. It was like the proverbial horseshoe. Chunni felt crest fallen. Did it mean that the attack will not go through?

The lack of success on the first day was a huge disappointment not confined to the assault task force alone, the higher echelons from Battalion to Brigade right up to Corps HQ were equally disappointed. They were all monitoring the situation and the progress of the operation or lack of it. The Left Shoulder was a thorn in the flesh. It was making air supplies to our forward posts difficult. Higher than all other posts in the surrounding area, the enemy post at the Left Shoulder dominated the area for kilometres all around, both by fire and observation.

It was decided that the search for the rope would recommence the next day. Viru passed the instructions on the radio set to all section commanders. The force was back to where it started. A false start indeed. Chunni and Laxman were heating their hands on the stove in their pup tent before having dinner, which was a bar of chocolate and some nuts and raisins. 'It is so disappointing,' said Laxman, 'it's like an anti-climax.'

'I don't know why,' Chunni said, 'but I feel more surcharged to find the rope tomorrow. I am confident we will find it tomorrow.'

'How can you be so confident?' asked Laxman, and Chunni simply replied, '*Mera dil kahta hai.*' (It's what my heart says). There is no arguing with the heart. The whole assault team wished to believe in young Chunni's optimism.

The next day, they did find the rope, albeit after hours of dogged and determined search. A silent cheer went up in the hearts of the Assault Task Force. They marked the rope well and decided to start the climb in the evening to avoid chances of being detected by the enemy. Chunni Lal was part of the first assault section that would lead the attack. Subedar Harnam Singh, the section commander, was a no non-nonsense man with a thin handlebar moustache which inspired the soldiers greatly.

They started climbing the near vertical wall of ice from the assault base to Saddle, which was to be the firm base for the attack. The ascent of over 1,000 feet took a very long time. The first few soldiers started reaching the Saddle only around midnight, having started the climb around 2000 hours.

It is painstakingly slow to haul yourself up with the help of a rope and an ice axe. Crampons were of tremendous help here. A crampon is a traction device with spikes attached to front and below the snow boots that improves grip and mobility in snow and ice. Rfn Chunni Lal was full of youthful enthusiasm. He was going into attack with his weapon slung behind his back, ice axe in one hand and holding the rope in the other, going into combat, the raison d'etre of a soldier's life. He felt important. He realized that this was a big moment in his life. He felt like a star. He was only nineteen.

The soldiers were climbing one after the other using the rope, but not too close so that if one fell he did not take the others down with him. One soldier did lose his footing. He slipped on the ice and could not hold on to the rope. He fell down several feet, and shouted '*Bachao! Bachao!*' (Help! Help!). Viru promptly growled back, 'Shoot him if he doesn't stop shouting.' That worked. The soldier stopped shouting and fell until he landed on a fold in the ice and a few helpful hands managed to steady him. Fortunately, he was more shaken up than hurt.

The Saddle Is Reached

As mentioned earlier, a Saddle is the little trough between two mountain peaks, and that is where their rope ended. Assembling at this Saddle was a very slow affair. Every few minutes one more soldier would climb up to the top. Viru ordered them to assemble in their section lots. The men started to take stock of their own loads, as also of their sections and groups.

There were several craters in the snow on the Saddle. These were formed by artillery or mortar shells during the exchange of fire which took place often between them and the Pakistan posts. Some were blackened due to the blast of the shell and some of the older ones had been layered with fresh snowfall. These craters provided excellent positions for soldiers to remain out of sight and for weapons to be deployed against the enemy. Under normal circumstances, soldiers dig trenches to keep themselves safe and for firing their weapons safely. Here, these craters would have to do.

There had been fresh snowfall recently and Chunni felt his snow boots crunch into the fresh snow at every step. It was a cloudy night and a strong breeze was blowing. This increases the wind chill factor. Wind chill factor can be explained as real feel of the temperature which gets significantly enhanced from the ambient temperature. In short, it feels much colder than it is. Viru prayed that the wind speed should not grow any stronger, otherwise it could blow up snow plumes. Viru ordered resiting of the fire base, as there was a crevasse where they had planned to deploy the fire base. In fact, Sub. Harnam who had had a fall into it, but mercifully it was not deep. But he did experience the extreme cold temperature and a twist in his leg. So the fire base was moved away a bit. What is a fire base? It is the place from where all the heavy weapons provide fire support to one's own attacking troops. Bringing down accurate and heavy volume of firing and shelling of all weapons on the enemy, the fire base engages the enemy effectively, leaving the attacking troops relatively free to attack fearlessly, albeit from a different direction. Needless to add, the fire base itself must be a defiladed position, i.e., protected from both enemy observation and fire, to ensure safety of men and weapons. For any attack to be successful, the fire base has to be very effective.

A big crater was selected as the fire base. Viru deployed a medium machine gun, two Light Machine Guns, one rocket launcher and one two-inch mortar. Havildar Darshan Lal was the fire base commander. It was so cold that most weapons did not fire. Rifles were firing but machine guns were not. The troops had to be exposed to this extreme cold temperature of minus 30 degrees for over twenty-four hours. Weapons jammed while firing. Several soldiers had swollen fingers which would not go around the trigger.

Captain Anil Sharma's section was to attack the enemy's Base Camp so that no reinforcements of men or resupply of ammunition could reach the soldiers at the Sonam Post. In effect, the purpose was to isolate them. Hence, the leading assault section was the first to assemble. It was planned like that. Those who were to start the attack were ahead in the order of march. Chunni was a member of this section. Subedar Harnam Singh was the section commander. A section normally consists of ten soldiers. However, it can be slightly more or less, depending upon the assigned task. For example, the requirement of cut off group was different than attacking echelons. They were yet to assemble completely and it was getting late and they feared that the attacking section could get daylighted, which could result in heavy casualties. Captain Anil Sharma, their leader was bringing up the rear, and the soldiers of the task force were still trickling in. Viru decided to start moving the first section, without waiting for cut off group to be in place, and to launch an attack on the enemy's administrative base. Waiting for cut off group to be in place, should have been the normal tactics. But these were abnormal circumstances.

The First Assault

With a prayer on their lips, the men comprising Sub. Harnam's section started walking laboriously towards the objective around 0330 hours. The altitude, the climb, the extreme cold and the fear of enemy observation slowed their progress. With each increase in altitude, the soldiers breathed more laboriously and their steps became shorter. Their progress was also slowed because they were crossing the ledge connecting the Saddle to Left Shoulder. The ledge was narrow, covered with thick snow, had treacherous slopes on both sides, and was slippery with snow. Moreover, the soldiers had been walking since after dinner last night but it seemed that they had been out for days. They were tired. Progress was very slow, but going slow was in any case necessitated for reasons of stealth.

It was also most important to maintain the element of surprise, as their survival depended on it.

The section had gone just a little distance, when the enemy opened fire using machine guns and small arms. The soldiers dived to the ground, or snow in this case, as they are trained, but Chunni did not flinch. He merely crouched to present a small target to the enemy. He was pleased with himself that instinctively he was not afraid of the enemy bullets. He thanked God for that. But his happiness was short lived.

The first few shots got Naik Tara Chand and Rfn Kulwant Singh, who were in the lead. Rifleman Chunni was following Rfn Kulwant and tried to pull him to safety, but it was too late. It was sad. What was sadder is that when our troops tried to return fire, most of our weapons failed to fire; Rfn Chunni Lal could feel a wave of frustration and helplessness go through his body. The weapons were jammed due to extreme cold, at minus thirty degrees or less, and some of the barrels had gotten filled with snow. It is not hard to imagine the chagrin and frustration of being shot at by the enemy, losing soldiers to their firing and, yet, being unable to fire back to defend your lives. How was the enemy able to fire his weapons then? Firstly, he was firing from the comfort of bunkers and secondly, they had stoves burning in the bunkers, as did our soldiers when we fired our weapons from the bunkers.

Even the artillery supporting fire had too many blinds. A 'blind' is a shell that does not explode on impact, due to extreme cold temperatures and cushioning due to snow, as the shells are designed to explode on impact on a hard surface. The supporting fire had not been very supportive. So many things were going wrong at once. This is called the fog of war.

The only weapons that fired effectively that day were from the observation post established by Capt. Ram Prakash near the post near the assault base. The rocket launcher from there brought down effective fire on the enemy post. So did the medium machine gun firing from the Garden Post. This effective fire support managed to maintain some pressure on the enemy soldiers.

It was utterly demoralising. Sub. Harnam's section crawled back to the safety of the Saddle, which was defiladed to enemy fire and observation. That means enemy could not see them, nor bring to bear the brunt of direct firing weapons. So, the enemy started firing artillery shells. Ironically, our soldiers sought shelter in craters that were formed by artillery and mortar shelling over the years, as they provided protection from shrapnels. Craters were also useful as weapon emplacements, from where machine guns and other weapons could be fitted at the enemy from comparative safety. Viru had made his Base or his HQ with his communication here at the Saddle from where he observed the progress of assault teams for most of the way till the top. He could also keep in touch with his sections ahead and the Battalion HQ behind on radio communication. Everyone including the CO, Col A.P. Rai, started referring to the Saddle as 'Viru Saddle'. An apt name indeed.

Meanwhile the day had dawned, but it failed to bring cheer. They decided to wait out the day and launch the next attack at night at an earlier time frame, before the weapons would get jammed due to extreme cold temperatures. Another interesting event of the morning was when one soldier slipped and fell down towards the Pakistan side in the wee hours of the morning. He rolled down about 70 m and was seen lying unconscious. When the sun came up, he regained consciousness and he got up. Then a three-man rescue party was launched under Havildar Bodh Raj. Using a rope, they climbed down and rescued the soldier.

Laxman Dass had been firing his weapon at the enemy from his crater for some time. His comrade Rfn Ram Singh asked him to take a rest break, 'I'll fire,' he said. The space available in that crater was so little that only one of them could use his weapon at a time. Barely had he started firing, he got a direct hit of enemy bullet on his bum; Rfn Laxman was wracked with guilt, for no fault of his. It happens often with soldiers in combat situation. The saving grace was that it was a flesh wound as the bullet had exited from the other side. Everyone comes with a pre-decided destiny and Rfn Ram Singh had to be evacuated.

In fact, several such casualties were taking place during the exchange of fire and shelling. It was critical to evacuate the wounded to medical facilities at the earliest, as in some cases it meant the difference between life and death. The wounded had to be brought down the near-vertical ice wall, which was a herculean task. The only effective way to do it was to tie the wounded soldier on one's back and half climb-half slide down the ice wall. The camaraderie among soldiers was at its best display here. The dare devilry of the helicopter pilots was no less, who flew sorties during the battle, braving the weather as well as the enemy fire to evacuate casualties to the Base Camp or the hospital at Leh.

The Second Assault

As the day wore on, some others also sustained gunshot wounds and a few soldiers suffered frostbite. Therefore, the composition of the assault sections had to be readjusted slightly, so that fully fit soldiers led the attack at night. Subedar Sansar Chand was the section commander. Havildar Ram Datt was his able deputy. He was a tall strapping young man, a wrestler and a very good man at heart. He belonged to a mortar platoon. He was the younger brother of Nb Sub. Ujagar Dass, also a wrestler and both brothers were a much-respected duo in the battalion. There were twelve men in this section.

The 'dirty dozen' set off towards the enemy post around 2100 hours. As they crawled forward, Sub. Sansar Chand was in the lead. This is the greatness of the Indian Army, the leaders lead, taking personal risks. The progress was very slow and painstaking. The ridge line was very narrow and there was a strong wind blowing. At one spot they had to go on all fours. Suddenly Sub. Sansar Chand's hand touched a boot. He probed further, shaking off the snow with his hand. The boot belonged to a leg. They had stumbled on a dead body of one of the soldiers of 2Lt Rajiv Pandey's Patrol.

Many years later Sub. Sansar told me, 'Mentally, I promised my dead colleague that I will take revenge for his death and I prayed to his spirit to guard over us.' Indian soldiers are very superstitious, and my battalion was no exception. They crossed more bodies, and with each salutation it strengthened their resolve—of revenge. Hav. Mulk Raj's body was found almost half buried in snow, in kneeling position facing the enemy, as though he was firing his weapon till the very end. Their weapons were also later found buried in the snow. The terrain and weather are so hostile, that the Pakistan soldiers did not dare to crawl out of their bunkers even to pick up our weapons. Capturing enemy's weapons is a big prize in the army, and yet, they did not dare. And our soldiers were attacking in such conditions in the face of enemy firing. Interestingly, I was told that 2Lt Rajiv Pandey's HMT watch was still working, despite the sub-zero temperatures. I don't know if it is true, but it made a good lore.

The assault section took almost two hours to reach the first bunker which was less than 200 m away. There were two Pakistani sentries on duty. As soon as they detected our soldiers' movements, they started firing with light machine guns. Our soldiers returned the fire, but not all the weapons were firing. Some were also jamming due to freezing temperatures, despite the fact that the attack had started earlier as compared to the previous night. Both the Pakistani sentries, however, were shot down. On our side, Rfn Tsering Narboo was also hit by an enemy bullet.

Unmindful of a fallen comrade, our soldiers continued firing to press on the attack. During the heat of battle there is no time to tend to the wounded, heartless as it may sound. The mission is more important. Even the wounded soldier understands this. So, despite his pain, his feelings are not hurt. Narboo died soon thereafter. This incensed his comrades.

Sansar crawled up to the bunker keeping a low silhouette so that enemy soldiers could not spot him. That was a daring act in the face of near certain death. Death of a fellow soldier is a great motivator and gives wings to courage. As he reached the bunker, he took out a hand grenade from his pouch, forced his frozen fingers to get circulation going because you don't want it to explode in your hands. He then pulled out the safety pin. Now the grenade would explode after four seconds. Subedar Sansar cautiously raised his head and body to a half crouch and lobbed the grenade through the loophole inside the bunker. They all heard a loud bang and then cries of 'Mar gaya!' and 'Ya-Allah!' Buoyed by this brave action, the rest of our soldiers rushed the entrance from the other side with their weapons spraying bullets, while there was still smoke and din in the bunker. Never give a chance to the enemy to settle.

Havildar Ram Datt, was not really a radio operator, he was an able mortar platoon firer, which was a highly specialized job. But he was doubling up as radio operator of Sansar Chand now to pass a message on the radio set to the assault task force commander, asking for 'Hero' and 'Pani'. Hero was the codeword for soldier and Pani for ammunition. In effect, he would ask for reinforcements so that they could press on the attack and capture the rest of the objective; but he could not get through.

He asked Ram Dutt to move by a few yards and try again. Sometimes, you don't get the signal at a particular spot due to screening, just like it happens with our mobile phones. Ram Datt was unfortunately hit by an enemy bullet and tumbled over to the spine of the ridge towards the enemy side. His body was never recovered.

Back at the Saddle, Viru's radio operator took violently ill. It did not look like he would be able to participate in the attack anymore. Viru was very fond of these two young lads from his Bravo Company, or Bahadur Company, as he used to call it, Chunni and Laxman Dass, from neighbouring areas of Bhaderwah and Kishtwar respectively. Viru asked Laxman Dass or LD, as he used to call him, to carry the radio set, and become the radio operator.

After receiving Sansar's message for reinforcements, Viru asked LD to get Sub. Sansar on the radio set. 'Bravo 1 to Bravo 4, over', LD pressed the pressel switch off the radio set and poke and into the mouthpiece. The VHF (very high frequency) radio is a one-way communication set. Only one person can speak at a time. That is the reason why a caller says 'over' at the end of his sentence. LD repeated, 'Bravo 1 to Bravo 4, over'. There was no response. Despite repeated attempts, there was no response from Bravo 4. Meanwhile, the sounds of firing from the enemy side were getting more and more intense.

'Keep trying from time to time to raise Sansar on the radio set,' Viru instructed LD. In their hearts they feared the worst. They did repeat this to anyone else that Sub. Sansar was not answering any more. Next, Viru called Bana, 'Take three men and try to establish contact with Sansar's section by moving forward.' It was a tough call, but a battlefield requires tough decisions and bold execution. Bana unhesitatingly replied, 'Right, Sir.'

'Be careful, don't expose your men to unnecessary risks.'

'Right, Sir.'

The remainder of the night passed in anxiety, punctuated by intermittent firing that followed the law of diminishing enthusiasm.

In the wee hours of the morning, Bana sent back two soldiers, who brought back mixed news. The good news was that Sansar's section had captured one enemy bunker but his radio set was not able to communicate. The bad news was that they had suffered heavy casualties. Sansar himself was not in good health. He was suffering from High Altitude Pulmonary Oedema (HAPO). He needed to be evacuated to a lower altitude soon.

Next day dawned, but the atmosphere was grim, despite the news of contact with Sansar. The enemy firing and shelling was continuing unabated. The men were getting sullen. The spirit was not weakened, but there was a perceptive dampening. In this harshest of environments, where weather was punishing and enemy bullets and artillery shells were causing casualties, our soldiers had been battling it out in the open for three days now, without having had a proper meal or a toilet routine.

Suddenly there was a crackle of static on the ANPRC-25 radio set 'Alpha 15 for Alpha 2, over.' The Tiger was on the set. Tiger is the code word for the CO, or a commander at any level. It was Col A.P. Rai. He had been getting the progress report on the operation through the Adjutant, Capt. Rajiv Maithani, rather than bothering the task force commander who had many important tasks to attend to. This was very mature and restrained behaviour from a CO. But now he wanted to talk. Why?

'Alpha 15 for 2, over', his operator repeated.

LD answered on a nod from Viru, 'Alpha 2 for 15, over.'

'Alpha 15 for 2, Tiger will talk to Tiger, over.'

LD handed over the handset to Viru, who spoke into the mouthpiece after pressing the pressel switch, 'Tiger here'. A task force commander is also called Tiger; in fact, every commander is called Tiger. You identify by the radio call sign or the unit or sub unit.

Col Rai spoke next, 'Viru, I am getting the reports, you and your boys are doing a great job in inhuman conditions. But I think things are getting too hard—weapons are not firing at night, we lost contact with our assault section under Sansar, it is tough for the resupply of ammunition to keep pace with expenditure, we have had far too many casualties. Should we abort the mission?'

Viru was in high battle spirits, though fatigued physically, 'We did not come here to abort, Sir. We have to avenge our brothers' deaths and we have to get their bodies home. We are going to give it another chance. Therefore, I think we must attack and take our chances.' He was adamant, but also making sense. But it was a difficult position for the CO to accept this and to order the progress of an operation at such great cost. I realized the enormity of this years later, when I was a CO in combat situations or as a commander in highest positions in operations.

Viru got his 'O' group together. The 'O' group at any level is the operational commanders group. In this case, it comprised Capt. Anil Sharma, the Cut Off Group Commander, the two remaining section commanders, Harnam and Bana. He left the supporting fire group commander to continue firing at the enemy. They reassessed the situation. For the third night in a row, they had been unable to capture the objective and had possibly lost Sub. Sansar's section as well. The men had been braving the enemy and the elements for three days, without a hot meal or toilet routine. They conferred together on the situation and came to the conclusion that they may not be able to last one more day like this, especially not another night in the open. Their weapons also don't fire well at night due to extremely low temperature.

A daredevil plan had started to form in Viru's head. It appeared as if Bana read his mind, because just then he too said, 'Let us attack during the day, Sir.'

There was pin drop silence. The sheer audacity of it! But the more the others thought about it, the more they liked it. Or maybe, got used to the idea of attacking Left Shoulder during the day. This would reduce their exposure to the enemy and the elements. Their weapons would fire because of warmer temperatures. Surprise would be on their side, as the enemy soldiers would not be expecting an attack during daylight hours.

These tactical and practical considerations were fine, but it is not easy to motivate troops to attack frontally during the day, more so after they have been out in the open for three days braving the weather, the terrain and the enemy. Even as they were discussing the matter, an enemy artillery shell exploded very close to the crater they were sitting in. They all ducked into a lying position. They had been saved by a whisker. An incredulous mixture of grief and rage swept through Viru. 'By God, we'll get those bastards,' he thought to himself. The decision to attack during day firmed in. There were no more doubts.

Rifleman Chunni, who was deployed close enough to hear the discussion, crawled up close to the Major and said, 'Sir, I promise, I will kill the enemy because of whom we have lost so many soldiers.'

The Major looked at his brave soldier fondly. It lifted up his spirits. And they made a pretty sight. It would have made a striking photograph, if there was a professional photographer with a wide-angle lens. Two silhouettes on the snow against the grey skyline—one a six-foot-two-inch tall burly Sikh and the other a five-foot-three-pahari Braveheart, a young lad at that. Viru gave a silent salute to the indomitable spirit of the Indian soldier.

The Final Assault

Naib Subedar Bana Singh was tasked up with five soldiers—Chunni was happy to be chosen for this assault. He was also happy that LD also requested the Company Commander Viru's permission, to let him join the assault; he was carrying Viru's radio set. 'I think I will also go in with the assault,' said Viru.

'No Sir,' said Bana. 'You will be required to coordinate all groups with the higher HQ and artillery fire support etc. I will lead this assault and you can follow closely.'

Viru said a silent prayer in his heart, Waheguru, *raksha karna*. (Waheguru protect them). Aloud he said rather gruffly to hide his emotions, '*Ya kabza karna, ya marna. Piche aaoge toh main shoot kar doonga.*' (Capture it or die. If you retreat I'll shoot you.). He said this in a positive motivational sense, not as a threat, and the soldiers understood that perfectly well.

The assault section stood around him. It would have made an interesting picture, an aerial shot, which looked awkwardly like the Indian cricket team's huddle, all dressed in white snow clothing, against the background of whiter snow. Normally they would've shouted out the paltan battle cry, '*Bole Jaikara!*,' (Hail Victory!) followed by '*Durge Mata ki Jai!*' (Victory to Mother Durga!) three times. But in proximity of the enemy, surprise is of the essence and pin-drop silence was maintained.

Naib Subedar Bana, Hav. Balwant and Rfn Om Raj gave covering fire, as Rfns Chunni and LD moved from a flank (from a side), crouching as low as possible to escape detection. Viru called for artillery fire support to cover their movement. He took the shoot himself. Taking a shoot means you apply corrections to the artillery fire by observing how far from the target the shells are falling. He passed the corrections on the radio set to the artillery gun position and expertly arranged for an air burst of artillery fire, which is most effective in suppressing the enemy. When a shell explodes on impact, half of its shrapnel gets embedded in the ground or snow. In an airburst mode, the shell is made to explode in the air just above the target—it calls for skilled shooting—and the shrapnel burst gets an enhanced range and effect. This is enough to keep enemy's head down for some time.

Taking advantage of this, LD and Chunni darted across. They crossed the bunker which had been captured by Sansar's section, also crossed over a few bodies of our fallen soldiers. They reached close to the enemy bunker. It was eerily quiet for a bit. Chunni prepared to log a grenade inside. He remembered Hav. Balwant giving him last minute instructions before they started, 'Be very careful, if the grenade falls outside the enemy bunker, you will die.' Very consciously, he pulled out the pin with his mouth, as he couldn't get his gloved finger inside the ring, and lobbed the grenade at the enemy bunker. His worst fears came true.

It hit close to the loophole of the bunker, but not close enough and fell outside. Both Rfn Chunni Lal and LD promptly lay face down in the snow and braced for the explosion. There was no time to do anything else. A hand grenade takes four seconds to explode. It seemed like eternity. They were so close to it and in the open that Chunni knew it was the last moments of his life, and he had only himself to blame. Even LD would die because of his mistake. He thought of his mother, how much she would cry when she hears of his death. His father would act brave in front of others, but would break down when alone. Time stretched even more. It appeared more than eternity. They couldn't believe their luck. It was a 'blind', it did not explode at all. What a relief. Finally, something misfired to their advantage.

Relief gave way to anxiety, how to proceed ahead? They were so near yet so far. How could they engage the objective effectively? Our own posts were engaging the enemy by machine-gun fire, and artillery shelling was intermittent. It would be ideal to throw another grenade into the loophole. But even if they threw in the grenade, there was a small risk that an alert enemy soldier could swiftly pick it up and throw it back at them through the loophole.

The training to beat that was an extremely risky manoeuvre, which is what Rfn Chunni Lal decided to do. He crawled very close to the bunker, pulled the pin out with his mouth, released the lever and held the grenade in his hand for a second and then pushed it carefully inside the bunker. This way the grenade had only two seconds to explode. No time for the enemy to throw it back. And their prayers were answered. There was a loud though muffled explosion inside the bunker. Their heard the cries of the Pakistani soldiers, 'Ya Allah!'

Enemy fire was now heard from another bunker nearby. During a lull in firing, it could be made out that the soldiers there were abusing in Kashmiri language. Chunni and LD could understand because they were from neighbouring regions of Bhaderwah and Kishtwar. They responded in kind in the same language. It also showed their desperation.

A profound thought then struck Chunni. 'After all the enemy too had been fighting a similar battle in the harshest of conditions for three days. If our soldiers were out in the open, exposed to climate and firing, the Pakistani soldiers too were bound to be feeling isolated and abandoned. No reinforcements could or would come to their rescue. It is a terrible and sinking feeling. Hence, their frustration was only natural.'

Meanwhile, our soldiers at other posts were able to spot a few Pakistani men running down towards their rear area. Rifleman Chunni later learnt that a couple of them had fallen to their death. The ridge connecting this post was narrow and riddled with crevasses.

'Oye Chunni,' Nb Sub. Bana called out cautiously. Rifleman Chunni looked over his shoulder, saw Nb Sub. Bana and Hav. Balwant closing in and gave them a thumbs up, signalling success. Relieved to see LD and Chunni well, they both crawled forward and joined them.

Now that they had exchanged abuses, the enemy soldiers were very alert from this direction, which must've seemed so unseemly to them for months, and they felt secure because of that. Now any amount of supporting firing from our posts would not distract them. Bana Singh, Balwant, Chunni and LD were in a fix on how to proceed across the few yards to the bunker. Frontal attacks are most difficult and risky. Our artillery shelling had stopped because our troops—notably Bana, Balwant, Chunni and LD—were on the objective in the open. Artillery shelling from the enemy side continued. The four couldn't stay in the open for long and survive and Rfn Chunni Lal suggested to his section commander, Nb Sub. Bana, that while the most risky move would be to attack frontally, it seemed the only option.

Surprise would be on their side, enemy would least expect them to do so. They also seemed to be low on ammunition, as their firing from machine gun was very controlled and intermittent. A man in such close proximity of the enemy would let loose belts after belts of ammunition, as he had adequate stocks. Their morale was bound to be low, because a part considered to be unreachable had been breached and they had suffered so many casualties.

Naib Subedar Bana looked at Hav. Balwant. He nodded. Then he gave a questioning look to Rfn LD, who gave a thumbs up. One shell landed a little distance away, and pieces of shrapnel whizzed close past them. There was no time to be wasted. There was also no time for prayer or a pep talk or a huddle, the customary rituals before an attack so Nb Sub. Bana just gave a thumbs up and they started crawling forward with a silent prayer in their hearts. It was a very audacious move, completely foolhardy.

They did not draw any fire from the bunker for a few seconds, then one short machine-gun burst came from the loophole facing them. But it passed harmlessly over their heads as they were hugging the ground and crawling in the snow, which saved their lives. At such proximate stages the defender comes out of his defences to fight a hand-to-hand fight, otherwise he is blinded inside. But the enemy did not seem to have the audacity for close-quarter battle. Our valiant soldiers did.

Hence, they crawled around the bunker and amidst more shells landing close by, reached around to the entrance of the bunker. It was blocked by jerry cans piled-up haphazardly. Chunni signalled to the others to stop and take positions, while he would lob a grenade inside. Soldiers always disperse and take positions rather than remain together, so that one grenade or artillery shell does not hit all of them.

Chunni moved closer to the entrance and lobbed the grenade after removing the pin. It did not reach inside the bunker, but fell clumsily among the jerry cans and Chunni ducked behind the corner of the bunker wall. Two enemy soldiers rushed out. From the other side of the entrance Bana rushed and shot one at point blank range. All others also started firing at the running soldiers. At such close range it was hard to miss. The enemy soldiers did not stand a chance. The scene got firmly etched in Chunni's mind.

Major Varinder and Rfn. Nek Ram, who were close behind, also reached and Nek Ram lobbed a grenade inside the bunker to clear it. He then sprayed bullets from his carbine to ensure that no one was left alive. It was unbelievable. It did not sink in easily. Then they all hugged. They did Bhangra. Suddenly their fatigue vanished. They felt like they were on top of the world. It also looked like it was the top of the world.

Post the Victorious Capture of the Left Shoulder

As the rest of the assault task force began closing in, enemy artillery shelling started again with a vengeance. There was no time to rejoice.

It was all about keeping themselves safe. Men took shelter in enemy bunkers and craters. Viru went around physically checking to ensure that everyone was tucked in and to reassure himself that no enemy soldier remained lurking somewhere. He was exposing himself to danger bravely and got hit by shrapnel in his abdomen. Suddenly Rfn Om Raj also cried out aloud. His right shoulder was hit.

Chunni and LD dragged Viru to a crater in the lee of a bunker and applied shell dressing—a medicated wad of compressed cotton carried by all soldiers, to staunch blood flow in the battlefield until first-aid arrives. It was tough to remove his snow jacket and warm inners to do this and after securing his wound, to dress him again.

Naib Subedar Bana and Hav. Balwant did the same for Om Raj, who was bleeding profusely. The dressing was not very effective in his case, plus his shoulder was also broken and rested at an awkward angle. He was evacuated using a makeshift stretcher, as he was in no position to walk. Four soldiers from the following section, who had not participated in the main assault, carried him down. They would be joined by others on the way. Evacuating a casualty in this terrain was and is a major, intensive operation.

Viru started giving instructions regarding coordinating and turning of defences. Soldiers are vulnerable after capturing an objective. They are open to a counter-attack and the enemy bunkers are facing the other way, towards their own side. Therefore, new loopholes have to be made, even obstacles erected if possible. Defences thus have to be turned and coordinated against a possible counter-attack by the enemy. Such an attack is likely in an early timeframe, when our troops on the objective are not yet fully oriented.

Here, though, chances of a counter-attack seemed remote given the terrain and altitude. Nevertheless, no chance could be taken after such a hard-earned victory. Viru gave instructions accordingly.

Rifleman Chunni urged him to rest as he had lost lot of blood. He took Chunni's advice and told LD to fetch Bana. Bana joined Chunni and LD to persuade the Major to go down to get his wound attended to. Once he sat down, Viru also started realizing how much of a toll the bleeding had taken, that too on the fourth day of being in operations. He felt very weary. Now that the mission was over successfully, everyone could feel the tiredness getting to them but he realized that he could not allow himself to fall sleep, lest he became unconscious due to loss of blood.

Before leaving he also cautioned all his soldiers, 'The tendency to fall asleep will be strong, but first you must divide time and duties amongst all soldiers. I will send reinforcements of fresh troops, but they may not reach till tomorrow morning.' It was 1630 hours already. 'Now we can inform the HQ that we have successfully executed the highest attack in the world and captured this post,' and with these words, Viru left for the Base. He wanted to go down while he could still walk. To see their commander being carried down is demoralizing for the troops. Viru, on the other hand, was a great inspiration for the soldiers.

'Congratulations and Jai Durge, Sir,' Bana said reassuringly. 'Please do not worry about anything.'

Next, Nb Sub. Bana took a stock of the situation and distributed areas of responsibility to buddy pairs, Chunni and LD were together. They took turns to be on duty. Yet they could not sleep easily. They could feel the cold seep in. Fingers and feet were swollen. Some had lost sensation in fingers and toes. The sensation of fatigue was overwhelming. What kept them going was the exhilaration of a stupendous victory and an enhanced sense of camaraderie between those who had performed this amazing feat of successfully launching the highest attack in the world.

Late that night, their first hot meal reached them. It was poori and rajma. Rajma is a favourite of JAKLI troops from Jammu and Kashmir, as it is grown there. The meal was a refreshing change and they ate it with relish. Meanwhile Capt. Anil Sharma, the second-in-command of the assault task force, had joined them by nightfall and had assumed charge in place of Maj. Varinder.

Around 0300 hours in the morning Rfn Chunni Lal finished his duty. Fatigue had set in completely and he crawled into the pup tent where Hav. Balwant and another soldier were already lying asleep. He squeezed in and they made place for him. Soon LD also crawled in and they made place again. Captain Anil also joined them and they all gave in to their fatigue and slept off tightly packed against one another, five in a space meant for two. It also kept them warm.

Early in the morning, when they were still asleep in a tight huddle, they heard someone calling out to Capt. Anil, 'Sir, the Brigade Commander is arriving soon.' That woke them all up and Capt. Anil went out first. He took stock of the situation and collected the soldiers who had participated in the final assault.

The Naming of the Bana Top

Brigadier C.S. Naugyal arrived and Capt. Anil saluted, 'Good morning, Sir!'

'Good morning, Anil,' the Brigadier replied cheerily, 'Well done boys, you all have done a marvellous job. You've done us all proud.'

He wanted to meet all those who had carried out the final assault. As they all lined up, he asked Capt. Anil as to who was the first to reach on top. When he learnt that Nb Sub. Bana was the section commander, Brig. Naugyal said, 'From now onwards this post will be called Bana Top.'

The Left Shoulder had been renamed the Bana Top. In fact, it was learnt later from the documents found in the bunkers that the Pakistani name for this post was Quaid Post, named after Quaid-e-Azam Mohammed Ali Jinnah. Such was the importance of this post. It dominated all other posts in the vicinity. And rightly so. The Brigadier's next words proved it too.

'A helicopter will make a trial landing in a couple of hours so that the top brass can land for themselves and see what a stupendous operation your paltan has executed. It was unthinkable until yesterday. This post did not allow flying of our helicopters, which was affecting our logistic sorties, which was the primary reason for this attack. And today we are thinking of landing our choppers on this post itself!'

While the trial landing was not successful on that day, an interesting development did occur. Most of the soldiers had an upset stomach because of eating poori-rajma the previous night, perhaps because they were eating a cooked meal after three days.

By mid-day, fresh troops arrived and our heroes were relieved. Rifleman Chunni's fingers were swollen and paining, so were his feet. Same was the case with Nb Sub. Bana and Rfn LD. Everyone had some problem or the other. Subedar Harnam's fingers had to eventually be amputated. Subedar Sansar Chand suffered from the beginnings of HAPO and had to be evacuated. They all had to be evacuated to Command Hospital at Chandigarh, some after a brief halt at the Base Camp, where they were welcomed as heroes. They all were relieved to hear that Viru's condition was stable. He'd had a miraculous escape; the shrapnel was lodged just a couple of millimetres away from his lung.

They had successfully executed the highest assault in the world, and more importantly, evacuated the bodies of their brave comrades

(2Lt Rajiv Pandey's Patrol) home after one month. That was the biggest reward for the soldiers.

For his unparalleled bravery, Nb Sub. Bana Singh was awarded the Param Vir Chakra, the nation's highest gallantry award. Subedar Sansar Chand was awarded the Maha Vir Chakra, the second-highest gallantry award. Major Varinder, Hav. Balwant and Rfn Laxman Dass were awarded a Vir Chakra each, the third-highest gallantry award. Rfn Chunni Lal and Rfn Om Raj were awarded a Sena Medal each, the fourth-highest gallantry award. There were more… the list of awards was long.

My battalion's lanyard was shifted to the right shoulder. It was a great honour and made every soldier of my unit stand out in a crowd. The suffix of 'Siachen' was added to my battalion's name. Thus, it became 8 JAKLI (Siachen).

We soldiers serve with the concept of unlimited liability. When a soldier goes into the battlefield, he is prepared to die for his country, for the mission, for his comrades. Yet we always have more volunteers than we need to participate in high-risk operations.

6
Attack Aftermath at the Siachen

AFTER THE USUAL debrief, all soldiers were taken for a medical check-up. Like many others, Rfn Chunni Lal's toes had suffered frostbite due to overexposure and not being able to change socks for several days. Despite the good quality of Koflach snow boots, over a period of time, some small quantities of snow had managed to sneak into his boots. When afflicted with frostbite, Chunni Lal had a feeling of numbness in his toes and had a tingling sensation in a couple of his fingers. During the heat of the battle he had felt nothing.

Severe cases of frostbite, if not treated in time, lead to amputation of toes and there were several such unfortunate cases in the unit. Chunni, along with many others, was transferred to Western Command Hospital, Chandimandir, near Chandigarh. At the hospital, Chunni shaved his beard. Soldiers could not shave at the Glacier. Paradoxically, now that they had gotten used to seeing each other with a beard, everyone was unrecognizable.

After he was discharged from the hospital, Chunni went home on leave. His parents were overjoyed to see him after a long gap. He touched his mother's feet. In most Hindu families, this is the way you greet your elders with respect.

Matrimony Looms

'How weak you have become!' was the genuine first reaction of his mother as she hugged him tightly, tears streaming down her face. 'Now that you are home, I'm going to feed you nicely—all your choicest dishes.' All mothers react like this even if the son has put on weight. But in this case Chunni had lost weight. The last few days had been very tough.

'I'm perfectly healthy, Maa,' he said briefly.

He touched his father's feet.

'May God bless you with good health my son.' Saying this, his father also clasped him to his chest. 'I'm so proud of you.'

'Oye Pyare, Oye Bipen, come here,' Chunni hugged his younger brothers. 'I'm going to take you with me to join my battalion,' he joked.

'Never,' said his mother. 'One son in the service of the nation is enough.'

'O Maa, Mother India needs all her sons,' said Chunni.

His father said quietly, 'My one son will do what hundred other sons put together cannot do.'

He then added, 'Kuldip's father was telling me few days ago that Kuldip had told him how bravely you fought the enemy at those icy heights of Himalayas. Fighting the mountains, the snow and the enemy at those high altitudes, you were leading in the attack on the enemy and were successful.' Kuldip was a soldier in Chunni's unit.

His father continued after a pause, 'He said this to me in front of the whole *biradari* (kin-community) when I went to his village one day. My chest swelled so much with pride, I felt it would burst.' He hugged Chunni again as tears welled-up in his eyes.

The next day, his mother said to him, 'Many proposals are coming for my son. I have started shortlisting a few. You tell me your choice, my son.'

Chunni replied, 'Maa, my life will be spent in my battalion, serving Mother India. Why do you want to spoil a poor girl's life?'

His father spoke gently, 'Don't soldiers get married? Duty is duty, family is family.'

'If you both insist, then you go ahead and select the girl. I will obey my parents' choice. I always have. You know what is best for me.' The brave warrior and an almost reckless soldier, was an obedient son.

His mother was moved to tears with the simplicity and obedience of her son, despite being a brave soldier.

Chunni gave her a hug, 'Why are you crying now, Maa? I just agreed to everything you said.'

'These are tears of happiness, my son. I am the luckiest mother this side of the Chenab.'

Before his leave finished, his parents took him to fix his marriage with a girl from a small village called Draphara, about 3 km ahead of Southa, where he had studied at the Government Middle School. The girl's family were also farmers.

Paradoxically, though he had gone to 'see' the girl, he barely got to see her as her face was mostly covered by her dupatta. All he really remembered was a big nose ring and her little brothers and sisters running around the house with excitement. They were eight siblings and her name was Chinta Devi. Her parents seemed proud of getting a soldier for a son-in-law. The wedding was fixed for April next year. Congratulations filled the air: '*Badhai ho*! *Moonh mitha karao*,' (Congratulations! Distribute sweets!) was the chorus.

Returning to the Battalion

After completing his leave, Rfn Chunni Lal returned to his battalion to a hero's welcome at Base Camp. The unit was still deployed on the Glacier. In fact, the battalion had been expecting a riposte from the enemy, shocked as they must have been after the loss of the Quaid Post, now Bana Top. And attack they did, at another location called 'Ashok and U Cut' forming the Northern Shoulder of Bilafond La Pass. In September, Pakistan's Special Services Group under Brig. Pervez Musharraf launched this attack at an altitude of 19,000 feet.

Rifleman Chunni, among others, was not allowed to go up to the higher posts of the Glacier because his toes were afflicted with frostbite. He volunteered to go back into operations but was not permitted on medical grounds. Repeated attacks by the enemy over three nights were all beaten back. Indian soldiers had been aptly inspired by the fantastic, successful operation on Bana Top. The soldiers of the battalion were so inspired after the success of the Bana Top operation that it was going to be impossible to beat them.

This became the defining ethos of this 'Jangi Paltan' (a Warrior Battalion), as the events unfolded over the years. Brigadier Pervez Musharraf, who later rose to become Pakistan's Army Chief (and later, President), never forgot this defeat and launched the intrusion in Kargil when he was the Chief, to strangle the logistics (all supplies) to the Glacier. There too, he had to face defeat against the bravery of Indian soldiers.

De-induction from the Glacier

After this defensive battle, the battalion was de-inducted from Siachen Glacier and moved back to its location at Khrew, near Srinagar. The unit needed time for rest, recouping, training and medical treatment for its casualties. There were also poignant times when the battalion reached out to the families of the fallen heroes. Alongside all of this, the unit was also preparing to move to a non-operational area.

One day, all those who had participated in the attacks on Bana Top were gathered to discuss the making of a documentary film of the attack for posterity. Viru started the meeting by asking everyone to observe two minutes silence to pay homage to one Officer, three JCOs and thirty-three soldiers who had laid down their lives during their six months of operations at the Siachen Glacier. In those two minutes, everyone relived poignant memories of the victory over mountains, snow, the Glacier, the weather and the enemy, but also grieved silently the loss of their beloved comrades, whose supreme sacrifice had made the victory possible.

Viru said, 'Comrades, you all did a great job. I salute your bravery, the whole nation salutes your bravery.'

Naib Subedar Bana said, 'Sir, our paltan paid a heavy price.'

Viru said, 'I read somewhere, "freedom is never free". That is so true here. We have to guard it with our lives, if need be.'

This had a profound impact on the barely nineteen-year-old Chunni. It made a lasting impact on his impressionable mind and gave him an even more daring and courageous attitude for the whole of his life. An attitude that his superiors, peers and subordinates found so inspirational.

Corps Commander Lt Gen Sami Khan, PVSM, SM, held a special Sainik Sammelan to congratulate the battalion for the stupendous operations executed by it at the Siachen Glacier. In the army, a Sainik Sammelan is a special address to the whole unit by any senior officer. It is of great significance to the battalion. He began by paying homage to the fallen heroes, paid generous tributes to bravery of all those who participated or supported the operations.

Talking of the successful attack at Bana Top at the altitude of 21,153 feet, he said, '*Yeh toh devtaaon ka kaam hai, jo aap sab ne kar dikhaya hai*' (It is the work of the gods that you all have managed to do). He later presented a silver model of the Bana Top and surrounding areas as a trophy to the battalion, which is proudly displayed there and continues to inspire future generations of soldiers to date.

A word about the Pakistani soldiers guarding Left Shoulder. As mentioned above, this post was called the Left Shoulder (of Bilafond La Pass) by the Indian side, and Quaid Post by the Pakistanis, after Quaid-e-Azam Mohammed Ali Jinnah. This also shows the importance of the post to the enemy's side as well. Their holding the post did not allow any Indian helicopter movement in support of posts all around. As Brig. Rajiv Williams of our battalion, who was present (as a Maj.) at the glacier during the operations, writes in his book, the *Long Road to Siachen*:

> The Pakistani soldiers holding the post also fought bravely till the end and deserve a mention, as they too performed admirably and kept up their commander's expectations of defending the post till the last. Like good troops, they stood their ground and warded off the Indian onslaught for three days till they were exhausted and gave up before the Indian reached their extreme levels of endurance. These men were led by a Junior Commissioned Officer, Naib Subedar Ata Mohammad. The two survivors

recalled the bravery of the JCO. 'Naib Subedar Ata Mohammad was everywhere. When we saw the enemy climb towards the post, despite bleeding profusely after being hit by an enemy airburst, our Naib Subedar kept going around and assuring us that reinforcements would arrive soon. The reinforcements never came, but we stood out ground and delayed the capture for three days till our ammunition finished, while food and water were never even considered for our survival.[11]

The next year on Republic Day, 26 January, Nb Sub. Bana Singh was awarded the Param Vir Chakra. He is a living legend. Rfn Chunni Lal was reminded of the battalion song sung on regimental days in his battalion functions. The song was composed by a former CO, Brig. S.C. Katoch, as told to them by Col Virendra Kumar, VrC, when he joined the battalion...

'Door hato, ae duniya walo, Bharat Desh hamara hai'
(Step aside World, India belongs to us ...)

> *Vir to hum me char hue,*
> *Ab Param ka chakkar pana hai,*
> *Agla mauka milne par,*
> *Seene pe ise lagana hai.*
> *(Four of our soldiers have so far been (awarded) Vir Chakra*
> *Now we have to attain Param Vir Chakra*
> *On the next possible opportunity,*
> *We have to pin it to our chest)*

Brigadier Katoch's composition proved to be prophetic. It was only the second time after Maj. Hoshiyar Singh that there was a living Param Vir Chakra awardee. Subedar Sansar Chand had been awarded the Maha Vir Chakra. Seven soldiers were awarded the Vir Chakra and ten soldiers were awarded the Sena Medal. Colonel A.P. Rai, the CO was awarded the Uttam Yudh Sewa Medal and Maj. R.E. Williams was awarded a Mention-in-Despatches. The unit also bagged one Chief of Army Staff Commendation Card and sixty-nine Army Commander's Commendation cards.

All the soldiers in the first wave of attack were awarded gallantry medals. Rifleman Chunni was awarded the Sena Medal. He was the youngest soldier to bag the nation's fourth-highest gallantry award. It was time for the war hero to celebrate in style. He was going to get married.

Chunni Gets Married

Rifleman Chunni was married in April 1988. His mother was overjoyed when he reached home on leave. She was forever bustling about happily. Her first-born was getting married.

'Aren't you happy?' she asked Chunni.

'If you are happy, I am happy,' said Chunni.

'Then why don't you look happy?'

'I am like this only, Maa.'

The barat (wedding procession) comprised about a hundred persons in all—family, extended family, friends and friends of friends. The distance from his village, Bhara, to the bride's village, Draphara, was 7 km. They walked the distance on foot. Only the bridegroom rode on a mare, as per Hindu traditions. He wore the traditional dress and carried a sword, which suited him as a victorious soldier. Drums were beaten all the way. When the barat reached close to the bride's home they could see the shamiana tent and the colourful arrangements to receive them. The band started playing. The men started dancing.

The rest of the evening was taken up by the traditional village wedding.

Back home Chunni's mother was extremely overjoyed. She kissed the bride's forehead and while welcoming her with a traditional *aarti thali* (prayer with incense) and said, 'Welcome home. God bless you to give me a grandson soon.'

At night, when they were alone, Chinta told her husband, 'Maaji wants a grandson soon.'

'That is the normal dream of any mother,' Chunni replied.

'But what if it's a girl?', the new bride expressed her apprehension.

'It will be a boy.'

'How can you be sure?'

'I'm sure,' he said simply, then added, 'and he will make a great soldier.'

Chunni's thoughts were always soldierly. That was the only life he knew.

A Peace Posting

Soon his leave was over and Rfn Chunni Lal joined his unit. The battalion moved to a non-operational station—Kota in Rajasthan—where the troops got time to rest, recoup and conduct training to prepare for war. The routine was less gruelling but no less important. It was important for the soldiers to keep training for their operational roles. Hence training courses and training cadres[12] were conducted, and sportsmen and athletes nurtured.

Soldiers were also permitted to bring their families to stay with them at peace stations, and many availed of the opportunity and the facilities. After three years the battalion would again be moved to another operational area, where family were again not permitted. The infantry units followed this cycle of peace and field stations alternately. During these three years, Rfn Chunni Lal's battalion concentrated on training and sports, besides other administrative duties.

The unit had a rare galaxy of heroes. One Param Vir Chakra, one Maha Vir Chakra, seven Vir Chakras, ten Sena Medals. Whenever any dignitary visits any unit, it is customary to introduce the gallantry award winners to the VIP. During a visit to our battalion once the Brigade Commander, a tall officer from SIKHLI Regiment, Brig. H.C. Gangoli said half in jest, 'I get a complex when I come to your battalion on seeing so many heroes in one line up.' The whole military garrison put together did not have so many medal winners.

Rfn Chunni Lal was often singled out as the youngest hero. As the Sena Medal awardee who was junior in service, he used to be lined up at the far end of the line from Nb Sub. Bana Singh, PVC. He used to imagine how it would be like to stand ahead in the line-up. He always aspired to be a brave soldier in more operations and win a bigger medal.

'Agla mauka milne par...' (At the next opportunity...), he would think wistfully.

It was now three years that they were married, and Chinta Devi wrote to her husband with the good news that she was expecting a baby. Chunni happily went home to welcome his son. He was supremely confident that he would father a brave son. And son it was. He was born on 22 May 1991.

'We will call him Manveer,' a beaming Chunni said to his wife.

'Now I see my son truly happy,' said his mother.

'What are you saying, mother? Admit it, you are the happiest grandmother that Chinta gave you a grandson,' said Chunni.

Chinta Devi sighed contentedly on hearing this exchange between the mother and son. Her own son meanwhile started to cry. It was time to feed the infant.

Chunni was an indulgent father. But he would get frustrated at times that the child didn't play with him as he expected. 'It will take about two months for him to start responding playfully,' explained Chinta.

'Oh, I'll be gone by then,' Chunni replied with a twinge of sadness.

'That is sad, but just you watch, he will bring you good luck,' she said.

Chosen for a UN Mission

His son did bring him good luck. A few months later he was told by his company's senior JCO that another battalion of their JAKLI Regiment was selected to be deployed overseas in Somalia for peacekeeping operations under the aegis of the United Nations (UN). A few soldiers from his battalion would also be selected. As a young gallantry medal winner his chances were quite bright. It was a coveted deputation, and there was a handsome deputation allowance.

After Kota, the unit moved to Bhatinda for a short tenure. From there, the Battalion had moved to Assam in 1992 where we were deployed in counter-insurgency operations. We patrolled the interiors regularly to keep a check on unlawful activities, mainly of United Liberation Front of Assam (ULFA), a dreaded terrorist organization known for violence and extortion. Whenever actionable intelligence was made available or generated, we laid ambushes for terrorists who were armed. Although still a young soldier with eight of years of service, Rfn Chunni Lal was a veteran in operations and an inspiration to younger soldiers as a gallantry medal winner.

Sometimes over dinner, the younger soldiers would ask him, 'Sir, please tell us the story of your attack and capture of Bana Top.' Rifleman Chunni was generally reluctant. He would often say, 'I just did my duty. Remember, your duty to your paltan, your country and your comrades is of utmost importance. You must honour these commitments even at the risk of your life. Only then can you be a true soldier.' The soldiers would hang on to every word of his.

After another month, he was one among the four soldiers selected for this deputation. It was an honour to be selected. But he did not want to leave his battalion, the troops with whom he had fought a tough battle, victoriously. He wanted to seek his Company Commander's interview to refuse the deputation, but felt relieved when he learnt that after the year-long deputation to Somalia was over, he would revert back to his battalion. He breathed easy. Rifleman Chunni was in love with his unit, his comrades were his brothers. Like any other infantry soldier, he spent more time in his unit than in his village. He shared his days and nights more with his comrades than with his family.

All those who were selected to go on UN deputation to Somalia with 2 JAKLI were called in for an interview with the CO. It was a line-up of gallantry medal winners and made an impressive sight. Other battalions had selected soldiers who had excelled in sports or other fields, but in Rfn Chunni Lal's battalion, even all gallantry awardees could not be included—there were so many. Representing 8 JAKLI were four in all—Hav. Balraj, SC, Rfn Chunni Lal, SM, Rfn Palam Singh, SM, and Rfn Rakesh Kumar, SM.

Colonel R.E. Williams, CO 8 JAKLI, was also an impressive personality, a six-footer with an impressive military bearing. His last posting had been as Adjutant of the Indian Military Academy (IMA), Dehradun, a post for which officers were selected for such qualities from the whole army. He had also been awarded a Mention-in-Despatches during the operations at the Siachen Glacier as a Major.

It made an impressive sight—all the medal winners at the interview where the CO was briefing them. 'Congratulations for being selected to join 2 JAKLI for this UN deputation to Somalia,' he said. 'While it is a matter of pride, it also places a huge responsibility on your shoulders. You are ambassadors of our battalion in 2 JAKLI. Your conduct will determine the impression they form of our paltan, a most decorated unit that has been awarded the highest number of awards in one operation. Later, as you proceed to Somalia, you will be the ambassadors of the Indian Army and the country in a foreign land where there will also be soldiers from other countries in your UN mission. Remember, it is difficult to win so many awards including the Param Vir Chakra, but it is more difficult to maintain the high reputation that comes with such awards. I am sanguine you will keep the battalion flag always flying high. Best of luck. Jai Durge!'

These sentences had a profound impact on Rfn Chunni Lal. He was like a sponge that soaked up all good things. He made a silent resolve to act and behave in a manner that would do his paltan proud. Always.

Rfn Chunni Lal, SM, recieving the Sena Medal in 1987 for showing courage and fearlessness during the mission at the Bana Top in the Siachen Glacier
Courtesy: 8 JAKLI (Siachen)

A photo of the Bana Top, which got its name from Nb Sub. Bana Singh, PVC, and earned Rfn Chunni Lal his first medal—the Sena Medal
Photo clicked by Maj. (later Brig.) R.E. Williams
Courtesy: Brig. R.E. Williams, YSM

Rfn Chunni Lal, SM
Courtesy: 8 JAKLI (Siachen)

Chunni with his family in his ancestral village
Courtesy: L/Hav. Manveer Singh

Chunni with wife and son, Manveer
Courtesy: L/Hav. Manveer Singh

A studio photo
Courtesy: L/Hav. Manveer Singh

Family portrait taken during Chunni's younger brother's wedding
Courtesy: L/Hav. Manveer Singh

Chunni and his wife at his younger brother's wedding
Courtesy: L/Hav. Manveer Singh

Chunni and his family during a visit to Vaishno Devi
Courtesy: L/Hav. Manveer Singh

Lt Gen. Dua at Chunni Lal's daughter's wedding in their village. Seen behind the groom is Hony Capt. Laxman Dass, VrC, who was with Chunni during the final attack at the Siachen Glacier in 2007
Courtesy: the author

V. Adm. P.S. Das, PVSM, UYSM, VSM, FOC-in-C, Eastern Naval Command, interacting with Nk Chunni Lal; facing the camera is Col P.S. Khangarot, CO
Courtesy: 8 JAKLI (Siachen)

Maj. Gen. J.S. Bajwa, SM, GOC, interacting with Nb Sub. Chunni Lal, VrC, SM, and company. Also seen in the photo are (from the left) Col R.P. Singh (CO), Sub. Maj. Shobha Ram (behind him) and Lt Col Sean O'Brien (2IC)
Courtesy: 8 JAKLI (Siachen)

Hav. Chunni Lal, VrC, SM as Instructor at Officers Training Academy, Kamptee
Courtesy: 8 JAKLI (Siachen)

Another glimpse of Hav. Chunni Lal interacting with the Senior Officers. The officers often sought out Chunni Lal to speak with
Courtesy: 8 JAKLI (Siachen)

Hav. Chunni Lal, VrC, SM, receiving Vir Chakra award from the then President A.P.J. Abdul Kalam
Courtesy: 8 JAKLI (Siachen)

An official photo of Hav. Chunni Lal, VrC, SM at Officers Training Academy, Kamptee
Courtesy: 8 JAKLI (Siachen)

Lt Gen. Dua with Chunni's father and Hony Capt. Bana Singh, PVC during the unveiling the bust ceremony of Nb Sub. Chunni Lal, AC, VrC, SM at his ancestral village in November 2019
Courtesy: the author

Nb Sub. Chunni Lal, AC, VrC, SM
Courtesy: 8 JAKLI (Siachen)

Wife of Nb Sub. Chuni Lal, AC(P), VrC, SM receiving Ashok Chakra from the then President Praibha Patil
Courtesy: 8 JAKLI (Siachen)

Remember, it is difficult to win so many awards including the Param Vir Chakra, but it is more difficult to maintain the high reputation that comes with such awards.

7

Of Peace Around the World
Chunni Lal Goes on a Global UN Mission

In 1993, 2 JAKLI was selected to be a part of the Indian Contingent in the United Nations Peacekeeping Mission in Somalia (UNOSOM- II). The shortage of manpower in 2 JAKLI was made up from other JAKLI battalions. Each battalion sent a few NCOs. The CO of 2 JAKLI, Col Anil Malik (later Major General) was empowered to select the best among them and return the rest to their units. All four boys from 8 JAKLI (Hav. Balraj, SC, Rfn Chunni Lal, SM, Rfn Palam Singh, SM, and Rfn Rakesh Kumar, SM) were all gallantry medal winners, mostly from the Siachen Glacier operations.

When Col Malik saw the boys in an interview, what struck him was that each one from 8 JAKLI had a medal on his chest. He said to his Subedar Major, 'To the credit of the Commanding Officer of 8 JAKLI, he has put everything aside to send me all his medal winners. Won in the icy heights of the Siachen, a trip to Somalia was the least he could recommend them for.'

The Subedar Major replied, 'Yes, Sir, each one of them really stands apart, in confidence and bearing.'

Colonel Malik said, 'We will select all of them. Not only because they deserve it, but also because we will need such combat-experienced soldiers in tricky situations. Remember, in Somalia we cannot fire unless it is in self-defence. Oh yes, there will be many tricky situations and you all have the right experience for it.' He addressed the last part more to the medal winners.

Rifleman Chunni felt very happy. He loved being in combat. His desire to be where the action was, always shone through and gave him a self-assured body language that his superiors cherished so much and his subordinates looked up to. The four from 8 JAKLI were sent to different companies, so that each company could have the benefit of a combat-experienced soldier. Nowadays, every unit has a large number of combat-experienced soldiers because of repeated tenures in counter-terrorism operations in the Union Territory of J&K and in the northeast, but in those days, when it was early days of the Kashmir insurgency, there were only a handful of units which had combat experience.

The battalion was part of the 66 (Independent) Infantry Brigade Group, Indian Contingent, Somalia, from 6 September 1993 to 23 December 1994. The battalion was deployed in the Bakool region of Somalia, approximately 400 km to the northeast of Mogadishu, covering a huge area of approximately 40,000 sq km. The companies of the battalion were deployed independently, far from each other.

Rfn Chunni Lal adjusted most easily to the new unit. He never even spoke of his own unit, 8 JAKLI or his exploits. He always spoke of 2 JAKLI as his unit as long as he was there. His very upbringing and attitude saw him being entrusted with onerous responsibilities.

Needless to say, he did everything so well and with the precision of a well-trained soldier.

The battalion's tireless efforts resulted in confiscation of large cache of arms and ammunitions from the local Somali militiamen. The unit also contributed significantly by brokering peace agreements between warring factions as listed below.

Oddur Peace Agreement: 16 December 1993

There was an Indian brigade in Somalia deployed under UNOSOM-II, of which 2 JAKLI was a part. It was successful in its endeavour of bringing peace between the warring Hadama and Jiron clans through a peace agreement signed at Oddur on 16 December 1993. Inter-clan clashes, which had erupted in November 1993 had resulted in many casualties and untold miseries to both clans. Consequently, a large number of Hadama clan members had migrated elsewhere. At the request of the elders of both clans and the District Councils of Wajid and Oddur, UNOSOM-II (2 JAKLI) was actively involved in the peaceful negotiation process and also provided medical treatment and transportation to Oddur, to over 500 affected people.

As a result of follow-up negotiations, the historic peace agreement between the feuding sides was signed by the leaders of the two clans at Oddur in the presence of UN officials, the CO and Officers of 2 JAKLI, and other political elders.

Baidoa Peace Settlement: 30 November 1993

Fighting broke out between the Leysan and Harin clans in the Northern part of Baidoa on 19 November 1993. UNOSOM-II (2 JAKLI) responded promptly to the request of the villagers to bring an end to fighting. Village elders and chiefs of fighting clans and other clans were brought together, along with UNOSOM Officers, the Police chief, and members of regional and district Councils. UNOSOM-II (2 JAKLI) provided an escorted transport to bring elders and clan leaders together for negotiations on 27 November. Rfn Chunni Lal was always in the forefront, especially while making contact with the villagers or while providing armed escorts. His presence was sought after by his Company Commander. He too never left an opportunity to volunteer for tricky or risky missions. The situation was finally brought under control and a peace settlement was made on 30 November.

The battalion had also been involved in several welfare activities, such as purification and supply of water, road reconnaissance and repairs, airfield and runaway repairs, controlling the law and order situation, inter-clan rivalry, and controlling several civil clashes. More than 100 medical camps were organized during their tenure.

Rapport with the Locals

In Somalia, Rfn Chunni Lal quickly won the hearts of all in the unit and his kindness even percolated into the civilians of the area. One fine day a woman arrived at the gate of the unit. She had sold a chicken to one of the soldiers and had come to return $99[13] to the buyer of the chicken. The CO happened to be present and he wondered who this soldier was. A fellow who bought a one-dollar chicken, paid $100 and hoped the remainder would be returned later voluntarily. What an optimist? He decided to wait and meet this largehearted soldier. It was Rfn Chunni Lal. He came up to the gate to take back his money. Colonel Malik asked him, 'Why did you pay $100 for the chicken? What if she did not return with your money? That was not very wise.'

Rfn Chunni Lal just looked at the CO directly and said ever so simply, 'Sir, I could have lost $99, but that lady needed her dollar more,' and then mumbled, 'A risk worth taking.' Such was the moral fibre of this young soldier. No wonder then, that Rfn Chunni Lal was most successful in making contact with the locals.

On another occasion, sometime in the evening, the unit received the news of a local boy having been injured at one of our posts. Ostensibly, he had fallen off a truck. He was being treated by our paramedic JCO. Sometime around 2200 hours, the Regimental Medical Officer (RMO—the battalion doctor), who had been monitoring the case from the Battalion HQ—felt uneasy with the lack of confidence being shown by the paramedic JCO and said to the CO, 'Sir, I think I t will be better if I can get to the post as soon as possible to continue his treatment.' That meant an escort of ninety men and a number of vehicles. Nevertheless, all that was arranged in quick time.

The CO went out to see them off and standing next to the RMO was Rfn Chunni Lal. He had just returned from a patrol, but had volunteered to be in the RMO's personal protection party. He spent the entire night travelling and did not sleep until the doctor had revived the boy and ensured stable parameters. Rifleman Chunni was with the boy throughout and even boarded the chopper the next day to be with the doctor when the boy went to the hospital. The RMO had great confidence in him and vice versa. They made a great team and one local boy was saved from near death. Chunni garnered everyone's blessings. Always.

Rfn Chunni Lal was really sought after by everyone. Once Brig. M.P. Bhagat, the Brigade Commander of the Indian Brigade, of which 2 JAKLI was a part, visited the unit for an operational review. He spent several hours in the unit, being briefed by the CO at the HQ and visiting other outposts as well. Havildar Balraj, SC and Rfn Chunni Lal, SM, were detailed as part of his protection-cum-guide team for the day. Chunni unwaveringly manned the light machine gun mounted on the open vehicle for hours without accepting to be relieved for a break in between. It is strenuous to do so for a long time, as you have to keep your eyes peeled for any kind of trouble, and keep an all-round vigil.

He did such a fine job, that the JCO Assistant who had accompanied the Brigadier, was so impressed that he asked him and Balraj if they would be interested in a transfer to the Brigade Commander's protection party. It was a prestigious offer. Even the unit takes pride in sending their soldiers on such duties. However, Rfn Chunni Lal politely declined, saying, 'Thank you, Sir, but there I will only be doing protection duties; my unit needs me more. I can perform many challenging tasks here, and I also have a great connect with the locals, which can be put to good use in functioning of the unit.' Such was his dedication to 'his' unit. On many occasions Chunni surprised with his sage thoughts.

During its tenure, the battalion had the interesting distinction of being addressed by a Pakistani senior officer, Brig. Saulat Abbas. He was the Chief of Staff of the Force HQ of the UN. Rfn Chunni Lal was intrigued. He thought Pakistan was the enemy. But he soon learnt from his superiors that Indian and Pakistan armies may be adversaries, but under the auspices of the UN, both were serving together. Such interactions do happen and both the armies are very professional about it. He recalled how his unit had repatriated the bodies of the dead Pakistani soldiers with due respect, during their operations at the Siachen Glacier.

Return from a Successful UN Mission

On successful completion of their tenure, the battalion concentrated at Mogadishu and de-inducted from Somalia to gather in Delhi in December 1994. Colonel A.K. Malik, the CO was awarded the Vishisht Seva Medal. It was a memorable tenure for Rfn Chunni Lal, for he got a very different type of exposure and not least for the fact that he could make a meaningful contribution. He made many friends and admirers, not only in 2 JAKLI, but also among the locals in Somalia. For someone who did not speak much, he always made friends very easily. He was a great human being.

Upon the unit's demobilization from Somalia, Chunni went home on a spot of leave. He was looking forward to meeting his three-year-old son. He had missed him the most. He was equally eager to meet his parents, brothers and sisters and his wife. He was carrying gifts for all. On the bus ride from Jammu to his village, he thought about them and it also crossed his mind that his father would be happy to hear that using his savings from the UN deputation allowance, he intended to buy a piece of rice-growing land. Any farmer feels happy about it. And Chunni had not informed his family of his arrival. He was going to surprise them.

But it was he who was in for a surprise, or rather, a shock. While he reached home in high spirits, alas, there was tragic news awaiting him. His youngest brother Bipen had passed away.

'Oh Maa, what is all this? How did this happen?', he moaned.

His mother kept crying, unable to reply.

His father answered, 'He had taken ill and suddenly, the cruel hands of fate snatched him from us without any warning. I must have done some bad karma ...' he sobbed.

Although Chunni did not cry, but he was deeply grieved. All his joy evaporated. He was glum during this leave. The only bright spot was his three-year-old son, Manveer, who oblivious of anything, was happy to play with his father who brought him toys, although it would take him a few days to understand that this kind man who brought him toys was his father. He came home so rarely. This is the fate of many soldiers. They spend so little time at home that their children, in their infancy, have trouble relating to them. Before his leave was over, his son had started calling him 'Papa'. Chunni's heart brimmed with joy.

Taking on a New Role

He reported back to his battalion in the operational area in the northeast. The battalion was in the last year of their tenure there.

One day, his CHM called him and said, '*Mubarak ho*, Chunni, new role for you and a new rank too. You have been promoted to the rank of Naik (Corporal). Tomorrow morning, you have to report to the CO for promotion parade.'

Naik Laxman Dass, VrC, was the first to congratulate him, having been promoted earlier. They both were buddies during the Siachen attack and had become the best of friends. Laxman also belonged to Kishtwar, which was the original region from where Chunni's father had migrated to Bhaderwah.

After a few months the unit was redeployed to the Andaman and Nicobar Islands. It was a peace station with a difference. His battalion was working with the Indian Navy and deployed in an amphibious role. They had to train for their new role in ships and landing crafts. The soldiers were required to land at a beach which had been taken over by hostile troops and their operational task was to recapture it. Something totally different from what Chunni and the whole unit was used to doing so far.

The three-year tenure in Port Blair was interesting but non-operational. However, Nk Chunni experienced new manoeuvres and new places. The soldiers had to travel to Chennai by train and wait for a ship to take them to Port Blair. The ship took three days at sea. All their supplies were also delivered by ship. Many soldiers brought their families to stay with them at Port Blair but Nk Chunni could not do that. His wife was the only support for his parents, who were coping with the loss of their youngest son. Moreover, his wife Chinta Devi had given birth to a daughter in May 1997. Due to the exigencies of service Nk Chunni could not go home for his daughter's delivery. This also happens often in soldiers' lives.

Colonel P.S. Khangarot was the battalion's CO and I was the Second-in-Command.

Meanwhile, in the home state (now a union territory) of our soldiers, J&K, the internal situation was taking a turn for the worse. Terrorist violence was on the increase. Therefore, in the mid-1990s, a decision was taken at the national level to raise an additional five battalions of JAKLI to wean the youth away from violence and terrorism and channelize their youthful energies towards a positive dimension.

However, the existing nine battalions of JAKLI had to bear the burden of sending a nucleus of trained soldiers to these newly raised five units and new greenhorn recruits were posted to the existing battalions to make up deficiencies over a period of time. Resultantly, these 'older' battalions like ours ended up with nearly half of our soldiers as greenhorns. Naik Chunni's Bravo Company was to contribute soldiers to a newly raised unit, 16 JAKLI. He sought an interview with his Company Commander and refused to be posted to another battalion, 'Sir, I have fought a battle in this company and this battalion. I will not go to another unit, not now, not ever.' He said it with such a determined finality that there was no further discussion on it.

'Shabaash, Chunni, I did not expect anything less from you,' said the Company Commander.

'Jai Durge, Sir,' saluted Nk Chunni and did an about turn.

It is just as well that he took a stand against being posted out to a new battalion. New battalions do not get a chance to be deployed in operations for the first few years till the process of training and integration has been satisfactorily completed.

Meanwhile, our battalion received its movement orders to be deployed at the LoC in Poonch in J&K. The move was to take place next year. Naik Chunni and the battalion were made for each other. He meshed with the paltan well and the paltan embellished him. People like him and our paltan stoke up a positive spiral of valour. He was the right man in the right battalion.

The unit's move from the Andaman and Nicobar Islands, was via ship till Chennai. Dependent on good weather days, this was a time-consuming process. And the movement over land was from the southernmost part of India to its Northernmost state. But the troops were happy. They were especially happy that they were going to their birthplace.

The battalion too was born in the same place during the siege of Poonch in 1947. 'Born in battle, purified in blood,' was the apt slogan coined by one of our COs. The unit was going to be back there after half a century.

Rifleman Chunni Lal was really sought after by everyone. Once Brig. M.P. Bhagat, the Brigade Commander of the Indian Brigade, of which 2 JAKLI was a part, visited the unit for an operational review. He spent several hours in the unit, being briefed by the CO at the HQ and visiting other outposts as well. Havildar Balraj, SC and Rfn Chunni Lal, SM, were detailed as part of his protection-cum-guide team for the day. Chunni unwaveringly manned the light machine gun mounted on the open vehicle for hours without accepting to be relieved for a break in between. It is strenuous to do so for a long time, as you have to keep your eyes peeled for any kind of trouble, and keep an all-round vigil.

8

Golden Jubilee Tenure

In 1998, the battalion was ordered to be deployed on the LoC at Poonch in Jammu and Kashmir. The soldiers of the battalion belonged to the Jammu-Poonch region. They were also happy to move closer to their native place.

Since they were going to be deployed on the LoC, they had to go for pre-induction training to the Corps Battle School near Rajouri for a month before getting deployed.

'What is the requirement of pre-induction training?' Chunni asked Laxman.

'Whenever any unit is inducted in a counter-terrorism role, it has to undergo this training. The idea is to orientate the soldiers for their new role.'

'But are we not trained soldiers? We have executed a successful attack on the enemy at the Siachen Glacier,' said Chunni.

'That is true,' replied his friend. 'But, for the last three years we have been doing amphibious training like beaching and attacks across beachheads, which are very different kinds of operations. Moreover, many new soldiers have joined our battalion over the last few years since we captured Bana Top. We all need to be trained together in company, platoon and section groups. You have recently been promoted from Naik to Havildar, now a section commander. How many experienced boys do you have in your section? You need to train them together in patrolling, ambush and cordon and search operations that we will be required to undertake in the vicinity of the LoC and the depth areas. Don't forget, we did induction training for the Glacier also when we trained for high altitude and mountain warfare.'

After completing the pre-induction training at the Corps Battle School near Rajouri, the battalion was deployed in their new role. During this training NCOs like Hav. Chunni Lal, who not only had combat experience, but were also gallantry medal winners, were a great asset in training their sections and platoons. These are the building blocks of combat in a counter-terrorism environment, where operations are mostly at company level.

I was promoted to the rank of Colonel and was appointed the CO of my own paltan not long after we completed our pre-induction training and moved into our operational area on the LoC. It is the ultimate aspiration of any infantry officer to command his own paltan, and lead his troops into combat. I was fortunate to be blessed with both.

Pakistan kept attempting to send terrorists across the LoC. It was our operational task to prevent infiltration and if infiltration did take place, then to track down the terrorists and neutralize them in the depth areas. The soldiers were eager to get into real operations and prove their mettle once again.

'*...Agla mauka milne par, Seene pe ise lagana hai...*' Chunni always hummed these lines to himself when he thought of operations or combat situations.

This tenure in Poonch turned out to be an operationally vibrant tenure and enriched the combat experience of the troops. The battalion preformed exceedingly well in operations, set some new records, won a lot of laurels and earned praise from their senior officers and higher HQs. This is the mark of a good unit. Our battalion, 8 JAKLI, never wasted any good operational opportunity. Whether it was at the time of its raising in Poonch, or in the Indo–Pak War of 1971 or at the Siachen Glacier, it always rose to the occasion and proved its mettle. It was about to do so again and live up to its reputation of being a 'Jangi Paltan' (a Warrior Battalion).

Hav. Chunni Lal was an important part of it. He was among the few who had participated in maximum operations and whose presence in an operation was a source of reassurance for superiors and subordinates alike. The battalion was fully deployed on the LoC in company posts.

As mentioned earlier in the Preface, the LoC is an unresolved border between India and Pakistan in J&K. While an international border is accepted and ratified by the governments of both countries, an LoC usually runs along a defined feature like a *nallah* (a mountain stream), a ridgeline or a mountain spur, but at times also cuts across features and even villages. The steep mountainsides are full of step-fields in J&K's border villages, and are very picturesque when the standing crop is lush. However, the LoC is also prone to infiltration because the fields run right up to the LoC, and people have relatives across the line.

There is no fence or markers to demarcate the LoC. Therefore, for physical domination of the LoC on ground, both armies occupy posts on suitable high mountain tops that dominate the area around.

As mentioned earlier, a post is made up of a group of bunkers constructed at a vantage point, or a height, such that it can guard over the larger area that it overlooks. A bunker is like a very small and low roof room, most of it underground, which offers protection against enemy firing, and has small ventilators called loopholes, from where soldiers can fire their weapons at the enemy. Its walls and roof are extremely thick and can absorb artillery shelling.

Pakistan has a similar set of posts on their side of the LoC. It is at these posts that both sides exchange firing of weapons, and it is through the gaps between these posts that Pakistan sends in terrorists. It is our task to maintain the sanctity of the LoC at all costs, and to prevent infiltration of terrorists through the gaps between posts.

The posts are permanently manned and the soldiers deployed there live in the various bunkers on the post. It is like a self-contained community, a group of bunkers at vantage points to cover the area around by observation and fire of weapons, if need be. The soldiers live and fight there, train there, cook there, maintain their weapons, are stocked with ammunition and other stores that they might need. It is the best form of community living. The shared risks cement the bonds between soldiers even more.

All four rifle companies of our battalion were deployed on the LoC, two of which were in a high-altitude area, i.e., over 9,000 feet. It requires four days of acclimatization at lower altitudes to get used to the lack of oxygen in a high-altitude area. Including the two companies in these higher reaches, all our four companies were only accessible by foot. The soldiers had to walk up from the battalion HQ or from a road-head in cases where the road climbed up to some distance. The HQ was on the banks of the Mandi River. There was a mountain ridgeline between the LoC ridgeline and and our battalion rear boundary, that was defined by the Mandi River. The entire area in between was the area of operational responsibility of the battalion.

Companies and platoons occupied their positions and started to familiarize themselves with terrain and routine. Havildar Chunni Lal led several patrols and ambushes. '*Raat mein* patrolling *karne se* dinner *hazam hota hai, aur subah* ambushes *ke baad* post *mein vapas aane se* breakfast *ki bhookh zyada achhi lagti hai.*' (Patrolling after dinner helps you digest your meal and returning to the post in the morning after being deployed in ambushes, gives you a good appetite for breakfast), he would often tell his boys. Young soldiers would hang on to every word said by Hav. Chunni Lal, SM, not just because of his hero-like status, but also because he would always lead his section from the front. This is the single biggest factor for success in combat in armies the world over.

First Encounter with Terrorists

Within the first week of the unit assuming operational responsibility in Poonch, we had our first encounter with terrorists. An intelligence report was received at the battalion HQ that three terrorists had taken shelter in a house in a village across the river, just a couple of kilometres from the HQ. Major Rohit Sharma, who as the Adjutant was present at the battalion base, swung the Quick Reaction Team (QRT) into action, leading them himself, and asked for extra reinforcements to follow, so that the terrorists did not escape.

As the name implies, a QRT is always armed with weapons, ammunition, grenades and other warlike equipment, ready for any emergency as the first responders. A 2.5 ton truck was also in the stand-by mode, as per the standard operating procedure.

Meanwhile, I was spending a few days on the forward posts on the LoC. On being informed, I had also started walking back towards the encounter site. I had been informed that the presence of terrorists was confirmed, as they had fired a few rounds. The balance of the journey would take over an hour. Simultaneously, I also ordered the commando platoon called Ghatak, which was deployed a few kilometres away, to reach the village where terrorists were hiding, at the earliest.

Havildar Chunni Lal happened to be walking down from his post on the LoC towards the battalion HQ for the CO's interview, when Maj. Rohit's QRT left for the target area. His patrol reached the battalion base a few minutes after Maj. Rohit's team had left in two vehicles. The Subedar Adjutant (SA), Sub. Romesh Chander was in the process of mustering more soldiers to be rushed to the target area. Men were drawing weapons from the Kote (armoury). The Ammunition NCO had been ordered to bring small arms ammunition and grenades to the mustering ground, when soldiers were reporting after collecting their weapons.

Just as Chunni and his patrol walked into the battalion base, three 2.5 ton trucks (soldiers fondly call them 'dhai-ton') also rolled into the mustering ground to ferry the soldiers. The Subedar Adjutant was overjoyed at seeing Hav. Chunni's patrol—ten additional soldiers all armed, kitted and ready to be launched into battle. But Hav. Chunni Lal was more overjoyed that he was going to get a chance to participate in the first operation of the battalion in this location. He asked permission to go to the Kote before getting hand grenades issued.

'What do you want to go to the Kote? You already have your weapon,' said SA Romesh Chander.

'I want to withdraw a bayonet.'

When SA Romesh raised an eyebrow quizzically, he added, 'When I come face to face with a terrorist, I'm going to kill him with my bayonet.' Such statements and leadership style were inspirational for the soldiers.

Soon the reinforcements were on their way. It was barely a ten-minute ride.

'We should dismount 200 m before the target area,' said Chunni to the driver of the leading vehicle, 'so that terrorists are not alerted that more soldiers have arrived.' Experience in combat shone through in that piece of advice. They dismounted and under the cover of trees and undergrowth made their way to the riverbed. The noise of the fast-flowing river water suppressed any noise made by their movement.

They could hear sporadic firing from across the river, which was noisy enough. On hearing the first shot, strangely, Chunni's heart leapt with joy. It confirmed the intelligence report about the presence of terrorists and assured them of their first counter-terrorist operation in this location. Several times they had drawn a blank when the intel about the presence of terrorists was wrong or outdated.

Proceeding with caution, the soldiers crossed the riverbed and a couple of water channels in ones and twos to avoid casualties by terrorist bullets. They need not have bothered. Their position was defiladed (protected from observation and firing), thanks to the flat trajectory of small arms bullets.

The riverbed was full of round stones and some sand. It was June and the water channels were easily crossed, although one had to be careful of slipping on account of the slippery stones and the fast-flowing current. In the batch of soldiers moving 20 m ahead of Chunni, one soldier lost his footing and fell down in the water. However, nothing was hurt except his pride. It provided a light moment in a grim situation. Only soldiers can do that. A soldier ahead of Chunni also lost his footing in the water when a stone under his foot rolled, but before he could fall, Chunni stepped up and steadied him.

Major Rohit Sharma was a smart, capable and a brave officer with experience, having operated in counter-terrorist operations in Assam in a previous tenure of the battalion. When his team crawled up the far riverbank, they saw two houses amidst fields and trees. The local source who had provided the information regarding the terrorists, pointed to the smaller house with mud walls. The terrorists were hiding in that. The other house was a bigger house, built with brick and masonry, though yet incomplete.

The two houses were separated from each other by a 30 m-field in which a maize crop had grown a couple of feet high. Maj. Rohit's team crawled towards the bigger house, keeping the bigger house between them and the smaller house. This would shield them from any firing from the smaller house, in case their movement was detected or even from stray bullets.

Suddenly, the terrorists fired a few rounds. Major Rohit immediately cautioned his men not to return fire and the terrorists soon stopped firing. They must have fired at some suspicious movement, hoping that if there were soldiers they would retaliate with fire. Thanks to his experience the soldiers did not give away their presence prematurely.

Once inside the big house, Maj. Rohit divided his twenty men into five squads of four each. 'Naik P.P. Singh's squad will stay with me, we will keep a constant vigil from the first floor of this house on their house. The source has confirmed the small house has only one door and we can observe it. The other four squads will surround the target house at a suitable distance, from all four directions as the inner cordon, to prevent anyone from escaping.'

Subedar Pritam Lal, who was nicknamed 'Commando' for having been a Commando Instructor at the Infantry School said, 'Saabji, I would like a terrorist or two to attempt escape, so that I can kill him with my bare hands.' With such joshila reassurance, the inner cordon soldiers crept away to take positions.

The houses were in middle of step-fields rising into the mountainside. Soon, more than a platoon worth of reinforcements also reached, of which Hav. Chunni Lal was a part. The Ghatak Platoon was about to reach as well. Major Rohit was getting all the updates on his radio set. He asked for Chunni to join his squad inside the house and ordered the others to establish an outer cordon. Chunni had the reputation of an experienced combat veteran, that defied his age.

'Once the inner and the outer cordons are in place and we have ensured that terrorists cannot escape,' said Maj. Rohit, 'then my search party will swing into action.' After the outer cordon was also in place, he led the assault team and sneaked up to the target house from a flank (i.e., from the side) using the 'fire and move' tactic. In this tactic a few soldiers move forward and others take position ready to fire.

Meanwhile, from the first floor of the big house, a few designated soldiers had been asked to open fire at the windows of the small house to keep them suppressed. In retaliation, the terrorists started lobbing grenades and firing their AK Rifles. The assault team retaliated in kind, then darted forward and sought cover behind a partially constructed mud wall and a couple of trees. A few soldiers of the inner cordon had crawled their way into the next lower level of the terraced field.

Exchange of fire and transfer continued for some time, with neither side willing to relent. Chunni crawled to the edge of the mud wall behind which they had taken cover and operated round the corner to get a better view. Suddenly a volley of shots was fired at him and he happily withdrew. He crawled back to Maj. Rohit and said to him, 'Sir, there is some *harkat* (movement) in the window. Let us lob a grenade each in the windows. That is bound to shake things up.'

The Major decided quickly, 'You go back to your position around the wall, I'll go to the other edge of the wall. I will throw a hand grenade into the left window and on that signal, you lob a grenade in the right window. Rest of you be prepared to kill them if they rush out.'

Havildar Chunni nodded vigorously. Briefly, he recalled lobbing grenades in the loophole during the attack on the Pakistani bunker at the Siachen Glacier. This was a much bigger window than that small loophole. He felt surcharged with an adrenaline rush. Both Maj. Rohit and Hav. Chunni Lal crept towards opposite ends of the mud wall. Chunni pulled out the safety pin of a hand grenade and kept looking at the Major for the cue. The moment Rohit lobbed his grenade, Chunni followed suit immediately. Both grenades found the inside of the windows. They seemed to have found their mark as loud cries were heard.

The terrorists started firing at a fast rate. Heavy exchange of fire ensued from both sides. Suddenly one terrorist tried to escape towards the river below, by firing his way through the soldiers. Major Rohit, the closest to him, rushed to intercept, shooting him at point-blank range. If the terrorist had gotten through, he could have caused us more casualties. During this close combat Maj. Rohit was also hit by terrorists' bullets and fell down on the spot, having made the supreme sacrifice.

At the end of it, though all the terrorists were killed, a pall of gloom descended on the soldiers and Chunni felt devastated. He and the Major had taken one side each to start the assault. Chunni survived, but Rohit could not. Once again Chunni was overcome by survivor's guilt. This is a cross soldiers carry often, especially when they have been comrades for years and grown up together in the army.

Major Rohit Sharma was a very popular officer. The morale of the paltan plummeted very low that evening. There was no joy of our first encounter with terrorists nor any sense of achievement at killing the terrorists. Even I was feeling very low. It was our first encounter. He was our first fatal casualty. I could not sleep the whole night. Then I realized that my soldiers were looking up to me for leadership. How could I act despondent? The next morning, had all my men gathered for a special Sainik Sammelan at the battalion base and addressed them. Such addresses are called a special Sainik Sammelan.

'Yesterday we lost a brave officer who took a bullet in his chest while leading from the front, but all three terrorists were eliminated,' I said. 'His bravery also saved the lives of some of our soldiers. He is a hero. Our battalion has had such a rich history of gallantry in all our operations since independence. Look at what we did at the Siachen Glacier a decade ago. There too our first casualty was an officer. Remember how we covered ourselves up in glory after that, executing an attack at the highest altitude in the world, capturing Bana Top, winning a Param Vir Chakra, a Mahavir Chakra and a host of other awards, including Chunni Lal who is sitting here among you and was with Maj. Rohit in the operation yesterday. We are going to do it again. What is the best way to pay homage to Maj. Rohit Sharma? By ensuring that not a single terrorist remains in our area of responsibility.'

A grateful nation conferred Shaurya Chakra on Maj. Rohit Sharma posthumously. It is third highest gallantry award in peacetime, equivalent of Vir Chakra.

Havildar Chunni Proves Himself as an All-Rounder

A few days later, Subedar Major (SM) Jat Ram and the SA Romesh Chander came to my office before the evening interview and the SM said, 'Sir, Hav. Chunni Lal is on the interview.[14] He is a brave NCO. We have selected him to lead the CO's QRT.'

Not wanting to reject their proposal outright, I replied after a thought, 'Hmm, I feel he's too valuable in operations, as he proved himself yesterday also. I would not want to waste his experience by placing him in a QRT.'

Subedar Romesh Chander then said, 'Sir, I have another suggestion. Why don't we appoint him as Officers Mess Havildar for a few months?' Romesh was a bright JCO and in line to be the SM next year after Jat Ram retired. It was clear they were suggesting that Chunni would be better employed in operations if he was deployed at the base, i.e., here. I asked him, 'Why Mess Havildar?' it is always good to heed the advice of senior experienced soldiers.

'Sir, if he is deployed on the LoC with his company, he will be restricted to a small area. As yesterday's operation has shown, more terrorist encounters are likely to take place in depth areas, as our preceding battalion also told us. Our reactions to such situations will have to be from the base. Yesterday Chunni happened to be here. If he's the Mess Havildar, he'll always be here, ready to go into operations and give good operational advice.'

'Let me think it over,' I said.

After a few minutes, the interview began. Different soldiers were on interview parade that day, for different reasons. Many were proceeding on or returning from leave, several others were going on some other duties, training courses etc. This also ensured that, as the CO, I met all the boys personally and got first-hand feedback about things. It also gave them an opportunity to bring out any problems faced by them.

When it was Chunni's turn, I told him of the decision to appoint him Mess Havildar, he protested, 'Sir, I want to be in operations, not administrative duties.'

I replied, 'More operations will take place here, and we want the benefit of your experience and bravery.'

'Sir, but—'

I interrupted him, 'Not only that, it will give the officers an opportunity to discuss operations with you and take your advice. And it will only be for a few months till the unit settles down in the operational area.'

An opportunity to get more involved in operations worked as an incentive. The Mess Havildar is normally selected from among those who are likely to be promoted as JCOs, to judge their potential. In Chunni's case it would be killing two birds with one stone.

Operational (Mess) Havildar Chunni proved himself valuable in operations and surprisingly, in administrative duties as well. All the officers were happy to discuss the plan with him, even when planning speculative operations, which are undertaken when the intelligence is not definitive. Moreover, when officers discussed operational matters among themselves, by virtue of his duty, he would be present, he would be around. His keen mind too picked up great nuggets of intelligence and tactics from these interludes.

Havildar Chunni Lal did not let operations hamper his given duty of providing logistic support for officers. Even if officers returned from operations or posts at odd hours, they were served hot meals. If an encounter continued for longer durations, he ensured that all officers and men would get something to eat in-situ, during the operation itself.

In one operation, terrorists started firing at the QRT soldiers as they were reaching the target area. The soldiers had to deploy prematurely before the cordon parties could reach. They also retaliated, firing back to pin down the terrorists. The terrorists, however, dispersed in the rocky terrain on a mountainside covered with trees and dense undergrowth. Havildar Chunni arrived from the base along with Capt. Vinod Kumar, the Ghatak Platoon Commander, who just happened to have come down to the battalion base for some documentation. They assessed the situation. It was unwieldy, as the terrorists had spread out over a large area since the cordon could not be established. Havildar Chunni advised Capt. Vinod that a rather big cordon would have to be established to trap them, and then a painstaking search of the area would have to be conducted cautiously.

On his advice, Capt. Vinod relayed this feedback to the Battalion HQ, and two platoons from the forward deployment towards the LoC were ordered to move down from the north to ensure that terrorists did not exfiltrate back across the LoC. The Ghatak Platoon had already moved in from a flank (side). They would begin the search only after a cordon had been established that sealed all routes of escape.

Search operations in the open are risky and time-consuming. Different search parties were allotted different areas with clear demarcation. Otherwise, it could lead to misunderstanding and fratricide. The rocky terrain, trees and dense undergrowth adds to the difficulty. This is where superior training and efficient teamwork counts for a lot. Training together for years pays a rich dividend in such situations.

The operation lasted for three days. It was a messy situation. Eventually all six terrorists were killed, but the battalion paid a heavy price. Havildar Babu Ram, who fought the terrorists bravely, was shot in close-quarter combat.

During those three days, Chunni played a stellar role. He was a good adviser and a good reassurance factor for his superiors and subordinates alike. He was also a source of inspiration for the young soldiers. He realized that this operation was likely to carry on overnight, unlike the previous operation in which the cordon was laid around the house where terrorists were hiding. Owing to his experience, Chunni thought ahead and advised that logistic replenishments include ammunition, food and water. He himself went back to the base to organize these items after having radioed ahead his requirements. He also withdrew two 84 mm rocket launchers with ammunition, to tackle any terrorists who were in the open by firing the rocket launchers in airburst mode. The rocket launcher is a versatile weapon which can also break through a wall, should the terrorists be hiding in a house. There are different types of rockets for different purposes.

He also requested the SA to send some men with him.

'I think you already have adequate strength of soldiers in the operation,' said SA Romesh.

Agreeing, Hav. Chunni Lal replied, 'Sir, these men are required for a short duration, only to carry this ammunition, food and water to the teams deployed at different places. The teams are not in a position to leave their position in the cordon.' Such forethought comes with experience. The thought of carrying more rocket launchers also proved to be very effective in operations later.

During this operation, three terrorists tried to break the cordon and escape. Havildar Babu Ram and Nk Rakesh Kumar were covering that approach. With great audacity, Hav. Babu Ram and his buddy exposed themselves from their cover behind the rocks to block the path of the escaping terrorists. Babu Ram dropped two terrorists at close quarters, despite the fact that their guns were also blazing. In the bargain, he was hit multiple times. Instead of slowing down, he continued to fire at the remaining escaping terrorist, thus bringing him down as well, despite being grievously wounded himself. Babu Ram later succumbed to his wounds, but set an inspirational example of bravery in the operation in which six terrorists were eliminated. A grateful nation conferred Shaurya Chakra on Hav. Babu Ram posthumously. It is third highest gallantry award in peacetime, equivalent of Vir Chakra.

Golden Jubilee Celebrations

In November that year, the Poonch Brigade HQ was celebrating the Golden Jubilee of the Poonch link-up. In 1947, a siege had been laid around Poonch garrison by the Pakistan Army. The first CO of our battalion, Brig. Chandan Singh, was invited as the chief guest. The battalion, under his leadership, had played an important part in breaking the siege of Poonch. He was a grand old man, eighty-seven years of age.

Any unit would like to put its best foot forward in front of visiting dignitaries. So, Chunni Lal was detailed as Liaison Officer with Brig. Chandan Singh. Despite his age, the Brigadier was a spirited and sprightly man. He was very impressed by this smart, confident, well-built gallantry awardee NCO, who was a hero already. Chunni was equally impressed by the Brigadier. During the three days that he stayed and attended events and functions, Chunni accompanied him everywhere. He learnt a great deal from the old man, who recounted stories of the good old days in Poonch, when he had assumed command of the newly raised battalion called 8 J&K Militia.

During his travels in the gypsy to the Brigade HQ, he narrated to Chunni that the battalion was raised in Poonch in 1947 when the town and its garrison, both very close to the LoC, were placed under siege by the Pakistan Army for one year. They outnumbered Maharaja Hari Singh's state forces and by the time the Maharaja signed the Instrument of Accession with India and the Indian Army could be sent to block invaders, they had already occupied the key heights that dominated Poonch.

However, one Indian infantry battalion—1 Kumaon—had managed to reach Poonch led by a daring CO, Lt Col Pritam Singh, before the siege was complete. He organized the defence of the town and garrison, mobilized volunteers to construct a makeshift airfield, which allowed the Indian Air Force to open an aerial supply route. He was promoted to the rank of Brigadier and was given the charge of all troops within Poonch.

Chunni was fascinated, 'What an interesting story!' he said.

'Let me tell you something more interesting,' said Brig. Chandan. 'After the construction of the runaway was completed, many who owned personal weapons volunteered to undertake guard duties. They were organized as Border Scouts. This later became my battalion, our battalion. Several such volunteer forces had sprung up in the whole of J&K, and were grouped as a paramilitary force called the J&K Militia.'

Chunni was overawed. 'The one-year siege must have been a difficult period, Sir.'

'Oh yes, as a volunteer force, we had to fight with our own weapons and ammunition. The Army could not even feed us. Our jawans families used to bring meals from home. In fact, there were times when there was a shortage of food in all of Poonch. Since our unit was composed of locals, we organized grain raids across the LoC twice. We raided their grain stocks after harvest and brought back grain in bullock carts, along with their cattle and livestock.'

Chunni found that so interesting that he was dumbstruck.

Brigadier Chandan was recalling old memories so vividly as he travelled in the land where he was a young CO fifty years ago, 'During the raids, our boys started raising slogans, 'Jai Durge, *phar lo murge!*' (catch the chicken) That is how our battalion got its battle cry of 'Jai Durge'.

He ended by saying, 'Even as a voluntary group, and later as a paramilitary battalion, my battalion had played an important role in breaking the siege after one year. Even as a volunteer force, our battalion was awarded one Vir Chakra and five Mention-in-Despatches.' The pride that the old soldier took in narrating the bravery stories of the unit was infectious. The battalion was truly 'born in battle, purified in blood'. The grand old man further ignited the fire of bravery and josh in Hav. Chunni Lal, SM.

Stemming Infiltration across the Mandi River

During that three-year tenure in Poonch (1998–2001) the battalion dealt with several infiltration attempts from across the LoC, which were foiled by my Jangi Paltan. All the attempts were aimed at getting across the Mandi River line overnight. If the terrorists managed to reach the depth areas of Surankot across the river then they could merge more easily in the densely populated areas. They even had more local support in those areas. Thereafter their ultimate destination was the Kashmir valley or areas of Doda/Kishtwar. The soldiers aimed to eliminate them at the LoC, failing which successive lines of ambush ensured that the terrorists were daylighted in our area of responsibility itself.

The sons of soil were charged up and acquitted themselves bravely. Being locals, they were able to develop good sources and generate real-time intelligence whenever terrorists sought shelter in their area. Once actionable intelligence was available, my battalion moved like a well-oiled machine. The QRT would be despatched at the earliest to keep the target area or houses under discreet surveillance. Meanwhile, more teams would be mustered at the battalion HQ base. The josh was to be seen to be believed.

We always had more volunteers than we needed. Jawans who had come down from the posts to proceed on leave, would volunteer to delay their leave to participate in the operation. Some soldiers on sentry duties would call in their reliefs early, so that they could participate in the operation. Once Hav. Chunni Lal said to SA, Sub. Romesh Chander, 'Saab, the mess cook is always pestering me that he wants to go into operations once at least.'

At the Subedar Adjutant Post, Sub. Romesh smiled and said, 'tell him he is performing an important duty. He is taking care of the officers' nutrition, which will keep them fit to lead the battalion. His josh is commendable, but everyone has a duty to perform.'

Chunni Lal participated in several operations. I always felt very reassured when a few selected officers, JCOs, NCOs and soldiers were present in the cordon-and-search teams. Their experience and bravery worked as a positive reassurance factor. Chunni Lal was leading the list. He was like a good-luck charm, much liked and respected by all. He was always cool and collected in any situation. He did not panic. He also did not hesitate in speaking his mind, whether it was to the officers or even to me.

Chunni participated in many cordon-and-search operations. All such operations did not result in killing of terrorists. Several times, the intelligence (of the presence of terrorists) was either false or old. The latter meant that the terrorists had left before the search parties reached. Nevertheless, such operations were also time consuming, as all the drills and procedure still had to be followed until it could be established that terrorists were not there. It is not practical to record all operations Chunni participated in, so only the important ones are being narrated here. After a few months of being in the base, Chunni longed to go back to his company in the LoC and requested me, the CO, accordingly.

Another fact that merits mention here is that Chunni's third child was born in December that year, but the pace of operations and the role he played did not permit him to ask for leave to go for the delivery. Early next year, when the higher reaches were snow-covered and the chances of infiltration and operations were reduced, he asked his Company Commander, Maj. Vijay Pathania for leave to go and see his newborn daughter.

'Why did you not go for the delivery?' asked Maj. Vijay.

'Sir, with so many operations going on, I did not feel it right to go on leave then. Moreover, I did not want to miss all the action as well,' Chunni replied and smiled.

His Company Commander smiled back, he understood that Chunni, the father lost out to Chunni, the soldier.

After completing his leave, Chunni returned to his company post and was happy to be amidst his platoon comrades. They all grew together. A soldier spends more time in his company and battalion than at home. He forms strong bonds, more so when sharing risks and dangers together with fellow soldiers, in combat situations. Soldiers thus operate confident in the knowledge that a colleague will never let him down. On the contrary, he will even risk his life to save others.

Now, Chunni happily got into the routine of patrolling and ambushes. The soldiers all looked up to him. He was a hero, not only of Siachen fame, but also having participated in many counter-terrorism operations. On the LoC, patrols and ambushes went out every night, either based on intelligence inputs or on speculative basis. During the day they would deploy men on surveillance duties. In Chunni's company, the villagers lived and tilled their fields right up to the LoC. The same was the case on the other side in Pakistan Occupied Kashmir (POK).

In fact, the LoC cut through Manthar Village. People had relatives across the LoC. For most part, the LoC ran along the Manthar Nallah, for which one had to descend down the steep mountain slopes. The company and platoon posts were at a height to afford better domination for observation and also for firing of weapons. Therefore, the locals lived and moved ahead of the line where troops were deployed. Sometimes, while grazing their cattle the locals would shout across to their counterparts on the other side and pass messages. Despite curbs on the populace, it was not possible to keep a total check. All in all, it was a porous LoC in terms of flow of information. That worked both ways. Information about our operations could be passed across. Conversely, our sources could also gain information and intelligence about possible infiltration attempts by terrorists and their likely routes.

Major Pathania, the Company Commander, told Hav. Chunni Lal, 'I am glad you are back in the company. We need your experience as well as inspiration. Since you have been away for a few months, let me tell you that by now we have built up a fair amount of intelligence on the likely infiltration routes that terrorists can use and we site our ambushes accordingly every night. We also know their likely launch pads across the LoC.'

'Launch pads, Sir?' asked Chunni.

'Yes, launch pads,' said the Company Commander, 'some of these houses, which are bang on the LoC, are the notorious ones which terrorists use before attempting infiltration. They have a tie-up with the families and come and stay there for a couple of days, observing the area on our side of the LoC. It helps them understand the terrain, mentally mapping the possible routes that can be taken, defiladed places to hide from firing by our posts.'

'Then they must be moving around in the area to do that. Can't we fire on them when they are in the open?'

'They move around in the garb of graziers with cattle. We can't risk opening fire on civilians.'

'Some day when we are sure that there are terrorists present in a house or two, we should launch a raid to knock them off there itself.'

'That might mean crossing the LoC.'

Chunni replied slowly, 'Sir, the LoC is meaningless at this point. If terrorists can cross over from these launch pads, so can we.'

'I wish it was that simple,' said Major Pathania.

Chunni did not give up the thought. After dinner one night, as ambush parties were preparing to go to their locations, he discussed his idea with Hav. Laxman Dass, VrC, who was his buddy during the Siachen attack. Now they both were heading different ambush parties that were going to different locations.

'Your josh has always been difficult to match,' he smiled indulgently at his younger friend before parting ways. They had a task at hand. An ambush location could witness an operation any night. Chunni could also not get the idea off his mind that if terrorists could cross over from the launch pads, so could we.

I used to visit all company posts once or twice a month and stay the night at some posts. I also used to accompany some ambush parties during the night at random, once in a while. During one such visit, Chunni broached the topic with me. 'Sir, if the terrorists can cross the LoC from the launch pads, what stops us from stopping them in their tracks and eliminating them there itself.' Having been the Officers' Mess Havildar, he was well familiar with me, so he could speak openly.

I was bemused, but also impressed by his chutzpah. 'You keep these launch pad houses under strict surveillance, and generate actionable intelligence and keep me informed,' I replied. This imparted a new vigour to the two companies deployed on the forward slopes of the village leading down to the LoC.

Several months later, another such opportunity presented itself in the neighbouring company locality, where our posts and Pakistan posts were much closer to each other. It was, therefore, easier to keep such launch pads under close surveillance. It was winter. Snowfall had taken place a few times and the standing snow was about two feet. The altitude of this post was around 7,000 feet. While movement was slower in snow, but every movement of soldiers or civilians left tell-tale signs in the form of foot marks in snow, if one walked away from the tracks.

On being informed that intelligence about terrorists' presence at a launch pad had been received, I walked up to the post. Company Commander Maj. Yashpal Rana received me at the Company HQ and walked with me to the forward post. Subedar Balraj, SC, was the post commander and had generated this intelligence. He was a brave JCO and had won the Shaurya Chakra many years ago. The readers have already been introduced to him in Somalia. He briefed me.

'Sir, we have been observing five new faces in that cluster of houses on the LoC.' He pointed towards three houses on the LoC around 500 m down the mountainside, almost all of which was white with snow, though it had started melting in patches. Two houses were bang on the nallah that defined the LoC there, and there was one house in the field about 70 m behind at a little height.

'How can you be sure they are terrorists, and not just some relatives?' I asked.

Subedar Balraj replied, 'They have been moving around observing our area. By their dress, demeanour and build also they look the part and moreover we have confirmed from our sources that they are terrorists waiting for a suitable opportunity to infiltrate. We should pre-empt them.'

'What do you have in mind?'

'Sir, we could take a patrol bang up to the LoC to deny them the infiltration routes they seek. Or else we could nip into the house and take them unawares,' said Sub. Balraj.

'Hmm...,' I was quiet for a while, turning it over in my head for pros and cons. I then conferred quietly with the Company Commander for a bit, and said, 'but you'll have to cross the minefields.'

Subedar Balraj was ready for that, 'Don't worry, Sir. We know the safe lanes, even cattle walk on those tracks.'

I voiced another concern, 'What about the family that lives in these houses? We would not want collateral damage.'

'Sir, the family members sleep in the third house, which is behind. We will cover only the front two houses on the LoC.'

Taking a deep breath, I said, 'Well then, okay boys, let us plan for tomorrow night. The moon will be in the fourth quarter and we need darkness in the early hours of the night. Let's get the best men for the job. Keep the team small. You take your best ten men and ten men will come from Ghatak. Ghatak Platoon Commander Capt. Vinod will lead the operation. All soldiers should be volunteers for this risky mission. And get Hav. Chunni Lal from the neighbouring locality. He has been quite enthusiastic about this idea for some time now. His combat experience will also come in handy.'

'Sir, they all should come today itself and familiarize with the terrain and task. Tonight, we will keep the area under surveillance with night-vision devices and double the ambush parties on routes leading from there, just in case they attempt to infiltrate today.'

'Yes, good. Do that. I'll be back tomorrow evening. Best of luck.' I said and then left the post.

The men mustered at the forward post that evening, with about an hour of daylight to spare for reconnaissance. They were briefed well and understood the situation and the risks very well. They were all keyed-up to go for it. Chunni said to Vinod, 'Sir, why can't we do it tonight itself? Why wait?'

The Captain smiled, expecting this impatience born out of bravery. He replied, 'We need to be thorough with terrain and plan our contingencies well. I will be able to do that tomorrow with you all. The ambush parties for tonight will leave soon.'

The next day, Capt. Vinod and Sub. Balraj divided the men into three teams of eight, eight and six each and briefed them in great detail. The first two were assault teams and six men under Nk Pradeep were to remain pulled back a little, as reinforcement or for casualty evacuation. They discussed various contingencies that could arise.

I reached the post next evening, along with Company Commander. After confirming that they were all briefed and ready to go, rather, they were eager to go, I addressed them, saying, 'Boys you are all going for a special mission which does involve extra risk and I am proud of you for volunteering.' I was speaking softly because of proximity of the Pakistani post. 'I am confident that given your josh and the glorious traditions of valour of our Jangi Paltan, you will return successful. I can promise you that you will all come back. God forbid, if anyone is hit, Pradeep and his team will carry you back. But come back, you all will.'

I then said, 'I've brought a few bottles of Old Monk and a tot of rum will be given to each one of you who wants to drink before setting out.'

Most of them had a small swig as the bottle was passed around.

'*Zyada nahin, kahin snow mein slip na hone lagna,*' (Not too much, I don't want you slipping on the snow), I joked.

They all laughed. It is important to relieve the tension before going in for a risky mission.

'*Josh poora hai na?*' (Raring to go?) I asked, a trifle unnecessarily. They were all raring to go.

'*Ji*, Sir,' (Yes, Sir) they affirmed in a muted voice, lest it be heard across the border.

Subedar Balraj said, 'Sir, I'm confident we will get all the five terrorists.'

'Good, Durga Mata will protect you all,' I said, 'Jai Durge!' The safety of the troops is uppermost in the mind of a CO, who is like a father figure of the battalion. He is colloquially called 'the old man', no matter what his age.

It was fully dark by the time they left their post. It was a cloudy night but visibility was fairly okay, because of the presence of snow. They were all wearing Pathan suits (salwar kameez) as the locals did, to merge in, just in case anyone spotted them. This was the usual practice on the forward areas facing the LoC. The leading team was under Sub. Balraj, as it was his post, and he knew the area best, especially how to negotiate through the minefields. Naik Prithipal followed close behind. He knew the area equally well. They both were literally at home here, as both belonged to Poonch District. Rifleman Zalam Singh was another valuable member of their team. They were walking tactically with adequate gaps between soldiers.

Capt. Vinod followed with the Ghatak soldiers in the second team. Chunni insisted on leading this team. 'I know the area better,' he said. The men were walking cautiously as there were chances of slipping on snow and slush. They could dare not walk off the track, because of drifting mines due to snow. The previous month a Jawan from this post had blown a foot on a mine that had drifted due to slush formed by melting of fresh snow. His foot had to be amputated.

So, while the crunch of snow beneath your snow boots provided a more stable footing, the risk of the crunch turning into a blast was too risky. Besides, the tested route were always the safest routes.

Naik Pradeep's party brought up the rear. They were all moving as quietly as possible. The fast-flowing nallah was in close proximity to the Pakistan post as well the target houses. The sound of gushing water was enough to drown any inadvertent noise made by the soldiers' movement. The route was also defiladed from the view of the Pakistani post for the most part.

It took the teams over half an hour to reach the nallah. Sub. Balraj raised his hand about 50 m from the nallah, signalling everyone to stop. Everyone stopped and took position in a dispersed manner because if they stayed bunched-up they would make an attractive target. A burst of gunfire or a hand grenade could get them all at once. Chunni and the No. 2 Scout moved ahead to meet Sub. Balraj as had been decided earlier. They were to recce two different points where the nallah could be crossed, so that Chunni could lead the Ghataks directly to their designated crossing site.

They moved away cautiously in different directions along the stream to look for suitable placed to cross, ideally where they could use rocks to walk over without getting their feet wet. They could neither see the target houses nor the Pakistan post. The converse was also true, which was reassuring. Eventually, they found only at one place that looked safe enough to cross. Subedar Balraj let his team across one by one. It was decided that they would crawl up a few yards and wait for Capt. Vinod's team.

Chunni went back to guide Vinod's team, as they had halted some distance behind. It had been agreed to keep radio transmissions to the minimum as VHF radios are prone to interception. If communication was lost, it could jeopardize the mission. Chunni gave a signal to Capt. Vinod to move. They all followed Chunni to the crossing site and started crossing the nallah one by one.

Chunni was the first to cross. The next soldier lost his footing on a rock and slipped into the freezing cold water up to his knees. Captain Vinod, following close behind, grabbed the soldier's hand, steadied him, then pulled him up and they crossed. The rest of them followed, without any incident. Having reached the other side, Vinod and Chunni crawled up to where Balraj had taken position and was observing the area ahead. They were now very close to the two houses. They conferred and each team knew which house they were to tackle.

Both teams had rehearsed this in advance and they crawled towards their targets. Each team released two buddy pairs, one of whom carried a light machine gun that, deployed around 25 m from the house, would cover any escape routes should anyone make a break for it. It was not a classic cordon, but it would have to do. In any case, this operation had to be over quickly, one way or the other. They did not have the luxury of time.

The houses were about 25-m apart. Their doors were facing the nallah. Capt. Vinod and Hav. Chunni Lal closed up to the door of the house and another buddy took position on the other side of the door. On the Captain's signal, Chunni knocked on the door. There was no reply. After few moments he knocked again. No reply again. But after a few moments they heard some noise inside, a rustle of movement. They could hear similar knocking on the other house also. Chunni whispered to the Captain, 'I'll climb to the roof, Sir, and drop something through the chimney.' Vinod signalled he would also come along. They left the other two to guard the door and circled around the back.

Finding no way to climb up, Vinod stood on Chunni's shoulders and pulled himself up to the roof. He then pulled Chunni up. They crawled towards the chimney. All houses there have a chimney above the chullah or the hearth for the smoke to escape. As Vinod reached near the chimney, a fire appeared out of it. It seemed so surreal. They were suddenly lit up by the mashaal or torch pushed up from inside the house. The purpose was obviously to warn the Pakistani Army post of some danger. Instinctively, the Captain showed great presence of mind by snuffing it out with his bare hands. It was urgent, otherwise the Pakistani soldiers could react anytime.

Just then they heard a burst of automatic AK Rifle firing from Sub. Balraj's house and Balraj's party firing back. The presence of terrorists was confirmed. A shot was heard from the room below them as well and Chunni quickly took out a hand grenade from his pouch, pulled out the pin and threw it through the chimney. It exploded after a couple of seconds. The explosion sounded muted because of the thick roof.

'Ya Allah!' he heard a shriek. 'Thank God they built thick mud roofs to withstand snow and rain,' thought Chunni. This ensured the grenade could not pierce it, which would have been the case with a tin roof.

They heard burst of rifle fire below them. The terrorists were trying to fire their way out towards the nallah. The Ghatak buddy pair that was left behind, fired at them. So did a cut-off group 50 m away. Vinod and Chunni crawled to the edge of the roof and fired at two fleeing figures. One of them had been firing short bursts. The spark from his rifle identified his location and he made an easy target. He fell down.

The firing from the other house also intensified. Balraj had also lobbed a grenade and sanitized the house by firing with the help of his buddy Nk Prithipal Singh. A couple of cut-off groups were also firing. For some moments it appeared that everyone was firing at everyone, especially, as seen from their top perch at the roof. But everyone knew who they were firing at. However, the chances of fratricide in such close situations are high.

'Cease fire,' Vinod ordered on his Motorola walkie-talkie set. Suddenly, there was an eerie silence. Firing had lasted under five minutes, but seemed much longer. Every bullet, every second could cause someone's death.

'What's your report?', he asked Balraj.

'Two down, Sir.'

'Own troops okay?', he enquired.

'Yes, Sir,' said Balraj.

'Let's go down Chunni and you check your team also,' said Vinod.

They took five to seven minutes in the dark to establish that all the soldiers were absolutely unhurt and five terrorists were killed, one by the grenade blast in the house itself and the rest while trying to escape.

Subedar Balraj said, 'It is surprising that the Pakistan Army posts have not reacted so far. Let us make haste before they do, Sir.'

As if on cue, a Pakistan Army post started firing in their direction. All soldiers took to the ground. They all were loosely spread around between the two houses, which provided some protection from enemy bullets for now.

Chunni said, 'Let's quickly search the houses for weapons and ammunition and look for the terrorists' weapons.' Two teams were quickly dispatched to search the houses. Four buddy pairs were sent towards where terrorists had tried to escape.

In all they recovered four haversacks filled with ammunition, grenades, medicines, clothes and some ration items; they also recovered three AK Rifles. The contents of the haversacks, especially food items, were indicative of the fact the terrorists were likely to infiltrate further the next day. They could be waiting for a guide or for instructions to move.

Subedar Balraj wanted to look for more, but Capt. Vinod vetoed it. 'We need to return immediately before enemy reaction is upgraded.' Getting into the nallah, they were defiladed to enemy firing and most of the path back to their own post after that was on reverse slope, hence safe from enemy small arms flat trajectory fire. However, if the enemy started firing with mortars, they could be in trouble.

So, they quickly retraced their steps, taking care not to bunch up. In the distance, from down-slope now they could also hear that the next enemy post had started firing. But it was too far to be a viable threat.

'Let's cross our fingers, and hurry up without bunching up,' said Capt. Vinod. 'Stay dispersed,' he ordered.

Their return was under enemy fire, but fortune favours the brave, and the entire lot reached back unharmed. Captain Vinod reported completion to me; I was waiting at our own forward post along with the Company Commander. It was an unbelievably quick operation. I was so relieved that all our boys were safe, without even a scratch.

I addressed the Jawans. 'Well done boys. I am proud of you all. I see that you bought some souvenirs too.'

'Sir, the weapons and haversacks of terrorists have crossed the LoC, albeit without their masters,' quipped Chunni.

Everyone laughed.

In a good operation like this, they were bound to bag some medals. The happiest part was that all the soldiers were absolutely unhurt. For soldiers, that is the best reward. They were justifiably in high spirits.

'Do give them a good Barakhana tomorrow,' I said to Rana. A well-deserved party. It's only traditional when any company or platoon excels at anything.

After completing his leave, Chunni returned to his company post and was happy to be amidst his platoon comrades. They all grew together. A soldier spends more time in his company and battalion than at home. He forms strong bonds, more so when sharing risks and dangers together with fellow soldiers, in combat situations. Soldiers thus operate confident in the knowledge that a colleague will never let him down. On the contrary, he will even risk his life to save others.

9

The Tathawade Operation

It was the month of June. The standing crop of maize was around 4 to 5 feet high or more. The region was known for maize and it was widely cultivated there. This was a nightmare for the soldiers. The crop offered cover to the terrorists to move around and even to stay and hide. It also offered sustenance once the corn cobs started growing on them.

The month of June had a special significance for Chunni. It was in June that he had formed part of the assault section that had executed the highest attack on the world at the Siachen Glacier over a decade ago. Then Nb Sub. Bana Singh was awarded the Param Vir Chakra, and Chunni was awarded the Sena Medal and there were many other awards. But he had also lost many comrades. It was on 17 June 1998 that our unit had the first encounter with terrorists in this area itself and we had lost Maj. Rohit Sharma. Now, it was June again. This standing maize crop had made the environment prone to anti-terrorist operations. Utmost caution had to be exercised, especially while patrolling the countryside.

On the morning of 16 June 2000, a reliable source came to the battalion HQ and informed about the presence of five armed terrorists who had sought shelter in a house in the village near the tactical HQ of the battalion. It was an hour's drive away from the battalion base. Thereafter, all movement towards the LoC was on foot. The source further added that the terrorists seemed to have infiltrated the LoC the previous night and were moving slowly, as one of them was limping. At daybreak they had entered a house forcibly and had taken the whole family hostage.

It was the normal modus operandi. No one would be allowed to go out so that no information about them could be leaked. And the family would have to cook for them. The owner had managed to get his elder son to slip out through a window. The boy went running to the source, who in turn, had rushed to inform the army. There were no mobile phones in J&K in those days.

Usually, the Army was happy to get timely and exact information of terrorist locations. But this information had me perturbed. If this was true then they must have infiltrated through our ambush parties. It was, therefore, all the more important that we track and eliminate these terrorists, lest they wreak havoc on the hapless public.

I dispatched three teams to include the Ghatak Platoon to establish the cordon and carry out the raid. Meanwhile, I also ordered some redeployments on the LoC to ensure that these terrorists could not escape and exfiltrate back across the LoC to avoid contact. I was being overcautious; it was good to cover all possibilities.

By the time the teams reached the target area, and cordon was being established, a man came running across the field towards them, waving his arms wildly over his head. He was the owner of the house where the terrorists were hiding, as per their information. However, he ran to tell them that after eating a meal, which his wife was forced to cook for them, the terrorists had left.

This was not unusual. Terrorists changed their resting place often, as they could not trust the villagers, unless they had sought refuge with a known over-ground worker or sympathizer. The teams were disappointed. But it was nothing new. More search operations than not failed to convert into an encounter with terrorists. Quite often the intelligence was faulty. Sometimes it was too late to act or sometimes it was wrong input provided due to animosity between the villagers. However, I was very disturbed when I was informed.

I discussed this with my Second-in-Command, Maj. Pradeep Tathawade, 'Pradeep, I'm concerned that these terrorists have infiltrated through our area of responsibility. We had a chance to get those bastards, but they have given us the slip again.'

Major Tathawade replied, 'Not yet, Sir. They are still in our area of responsibility. They have not yet crossed the Mandi River line, which is our rear boundary."

'Yes, of course. We will deploy more troops and teams and ferret them out,' I said determinedly. 'Teams will start combing the area from the LoC southwards and from the base northwards. Ghataks will cover the western side. There are not likely to climb the higher heights towards the East as the high-altitude ridges are devoid of any tree cover and inhabitation. Still, we will send a cut-off group from Bravo Company to cover that side."

'Sir, it will be dark soon,' said Pradeep.

'Yes, we will begin the search operations at first light tomorrow morning. For the night, all teams will lay ambushes on the likely escape routes in their respective areas to seal them in.'

'Sir, I will go to the Tactical HQ and control the search operations from there,' Pradeep volunteered.

'Best of luck, Pradeep. Don't let the bastards get away. Keep me posted,' I said.

By nightfall all teams were deployed in ambush mode. Major Pradeep reached the Tac HQ and took reports from all team leaders on the radio set. All villagers had been informed not to move out at night as the army's ambush parties could mistake them for terrorists. As it is, there was a night curfew in the vicinity of the LoC. The implication was that the Army soldiers were well within their rights to open fire at any surreptitious movement at night. All intelligence sources had been informed to report to the Tac HQ or the nearest Army team, if they learnt anything about terrorist movement.

It was an uneasy night for everyone. As the CO, I kept waiting to hear reports of a contact, and Pradeep kept hoping to get some intelligence on movement of terrorists, while the soldiers in the teams deployed in the large area of mountainside kept their eyes and ears peeled for any suspicious movement. The terrorists too must be spending a sleepless night. But where?

The first glow of the morning, even before the sun was up, brought a spot of bright news. One of the villagers turned up at the Tac HQ and informed them that the terrorists were hiding in a dhok in his fields. A dhok is a temporary house in the higher reaches that the villagers use when they bring their cattle there for grazing.

Pradeep was excited. Based on the villager's description, he ordered the teams to close in towards the target house and lay a bigger cordon than usual and started walking towards the target house with his QRT. He had already informed me of the news on telephone before leaving.

'All the best, Pradeep. Be careful. I will also start immediately from here but it will take me about an hour to reach there.'

Havildar Chunni Lal was a part of the team that had descended from the LoC posts. Major Pradeep's team had to descend from the road-head in a re-entrant[15]. It was a clear day and sun was shining in the sky. The area was full of dense bushes and shrubs. The soldiers were moving cautiously using their cover. Being June, the soldiers were dressed lightly. It was a clear day, and a crisp morning. Major Pradeep issued orders on the radio set for a few experienced JCOs and NCOs to meet his team near the target house. It included Chunni, Sub. Bodh Raj and Sub. Pritam, also known as 'Commando'. With their help, Maj. Pradeep adjusted the cordon to ensure that the terrorists would not be able to escape.

Led by Maj. Pradeep, the assault team crawled cautiously towards the house, moving from cover to cover. Major Pradeep silently prayed that the information provided by the local was correct and the terrorists were inside the house. As if in answer to his prayers, a short burst from an AK Rifle erupted from the house and broke the early morning calm. Strangely relieved, he dashed to the ground so as to not present a target. It may seem ironical that he felt relieved, but this was because it confirmed the presence of the terrorists. It strengthened his resolve not to let them escape. All other soldiers followed suit.

They were all trained in these drills and did them reflexively. 'Dash, down, crawl, observe, sight, fire' was the sequence taught to them during their training, remembered Chunni. And this drill had saved their lives countless times. Major Pradeep and Chunni fired back at the house. They aimed for the windows. The door was closed. From the other flank, the commando's boys too were engaging the house by firing.

The whole valley reverberated with the shots and their echoes. The rest of the cordon parties held their fire. That was the drill. This exchange of fire continued for about fifteen minutes. Major Pradeep's position was below the house. It was a shallow re-entrant. The slope was fairly steep. He and Chunni had taken position behind a rock to shield themselves from the terrorists' bullets.

All villagers in the villages around in the valley would stay confined to their houses automatically. There was a stalemate for some time and there was a sporadic exchange of fire. Major Pradeep was in no rush. Their cordon was well in place. It was early morning, and they had time on their side. Suddenly they saw a flash of movement from the house. Through the bushes they spotted the terrorists trying to escape, bent low and running to make a break for it. As far as they could make out three ran down in one direction and two in another. This escape route was being covered by Pradeep and Chunni.

'Chunni you take those two,' shouted Pradeep and moved swiftly to intercept the other three. Chunni was calm. He rolled swiftly further towards their line of escape, took position, waited a few seconds for the two terrorists to close in and lobbed a grenade. He lay down on the ground to save himself from the shrapnel following the grenade burst. He then fired his automatic coolly into the fleeing figures. He was confident that he would drop them. And he did. He pumped a few more bullets, just to be sure. Then he heard the commotion.

Major Pradeep had not been able to get a good field of fire due to dense foliage. He grew concerned that they would escape. He had to take a split-second decision. Displaying utmost courage and throwing caution to the winds, he stepped away from the rock and took a kneeling position to get a better view to fire his weapon. In so doing, he exposed himself and made a shootable target. But his decision was totally timely. Two terrorists had already dashed to the slope below him. He fired a long burst of bullets from his AK

Rifle and had the satisfaction of seeing both of them drop. It was the first time that he had personally dropped terrorists. His felt a flash of jubilant mood.

In this mood he turned towards Chunni, but before he could shout out, from the corner of his eye he saw a dark shape hurling directly towards him. He happened to have risen to kneeling position directly in the line of the following third terrorist. Both were equally surprised. Before anyone could react, the terrorist collided into Maj. Pradeep. There was no time to swing his weapon towards the terrorist. So, Maj. Pradeep tried to catch him to prevent his escape. They both got into a bear hug and rolled down the slope for a few metres and Maj. Pradeep felt a stone hurt his hip and felt his hands getting bruised.

They would have perhaps rolled even farther down, but a big thorny bush in their path broke their momentum and they both were separated. Out of breath and badly bruised, they both swung their weapons at each other and fired. They were so close that both found their mark.

Chunni had heard the commotion, and after dealing with his targets he turned his weapon to help Pradeep, but he could not fire for the fear of hitting the Major while they were rolling down together. The moment they separated, Chunni heard them both firing. He also dived towards the terrorist, although he did not have a good view because of huge bushes with thorns in the roughly 15 m or so that separated them. Suddenly, there was a deafening silence.

Other teams also held their fire, as they did not know their exact positions. Chunni rushed towards Pradeep, who was groaning. He was bleeding profusely from his abdomen just below the bulletproof jacket and his thigh. The sight Chunni remembered most was that there was so much blood. The terrorist was lying close by, unmoving.

'O Commando Saab,' Chunni shouted across to Pritam, '*Idhar aana*, Major *saab ko lagi hai*' (Come here, the Major is hit). There was a ghastly gash in the thigh. Chunni tore open his back pack and took out the first field dressing, which is used to staunch blood in the battlefield. Pradeep groaned and asked for water.

'Paani,' he managed to say.

Chunni pulled out his water bottle and gave him a sip.

As though he felt a little resuscitated, Pradeep said to Chunni, 'Keep my leg with me. I can't feel it at all.' Only a brave soldier can use levity in such dire times. After that he passed out.

'You will be alright, Sir. We will take you to hospital right now. But congratulations, Sir. You knocked off three terrorists.' Pradeep did not hear any of that.

Just then, Pritam and the others reached. They helped staunch the bleeding but the earth below Major Tathawade was soaked with blood. They lifted him carefully, lifting his leg with extra care. The Battlefield Nursing Assistant (BFNA) rushed forward with a stretcher. Four soldiers carried him to the top of the ridgeline where the ambulance was waiting. These are standard drills in a battalion when any operation starts off. The unit Medical Officer was already on his way. So was I, separately though. I met the ambulance a few hundred metres after it had started on its journey to the hospital. I stopped them briefly, saw that Pradeep was unconscious and told them to hurry on. Every moment was precious, when the patient has lost a lot of blood.

By the time the I reached the encounter site, mopping up operations were on. After every encounter, the area around is searched thoroughly in a tactical manner, for any more terrorists and their equipment. Five bodies had been accounted for. Their weapons, ammunition, grenades, explosives, and other logistic stores, including medicines, were being counted. The five dead terrorists were also found to be carrying more than a lakh of rupees in cash.

I was met by Pritam and Chunni. Pritam reported, 'All our boys are okay, Sir, only Major Sahab is hit. Five terrorists eliminated.'

When the I learnt that Chunni was Pradeep's buddy during the assault, I asked him to narrate the whole episode. When he finished, I said, 'Congratulations Chunni, well done.'

Chunni replied, 'It was team work, Sir. They happened to run towards us, and we got to pull the trigger. Everyone has been on the operation for more than twenty-four hours.'

'That is true,' I said. 'It is this teamwork that sets the Army apart, and our unit excels in this.'

Soon, Maj. Himanshu Sawant too reached the site. He was in-charge of the cordon which was down slope. He started climbing up after the sanitization operation was over, as is the drill.

'Exactly two years ago, on this day we had lost Maj. Rohit Sharma, Sir,' Chunni recalled.

'Yes,' I concurred. 'We had scheduled a wreath laying at the War Memorial at the battalion HQ to pay homage to him. But I guess his memory would be better served by eliminating a few more terrorists on this day.'

Just then I received a call on the radio set from Maj. Sean O'Brien, the Adjutant. Major Pradeep Tathawade was no more.

Suddenly, a pall of gloom descended on everyone. Despite being the Second-in-Command of the battalion, he had volunteered to lead the operation. While he led the troops bravely from the front, leading by personal example, he paid a heavy price. This is the concept of unlimited liability a soldier serves with.

Chunni was overwhelmed with grief. He was with Major sahab in his last moments. They fought the terrorists rush together, and eliminated them. He had given him his last sip of water. Major sahab had joked with him about keeping his leg together with him.

'Rest in peace, Sir,' he thought. Aloud he said, 'Om Shanti.'

Yes, June was an ominous month for operations in the paltan.

Little did Chunni realize then that his own crowning glory as well as his end would also come in the month of June several years later. Maybe that is why he had a morbid fascination for operations that took place in June, starting from his first operation at the Siachen Glacier.

A grateful nation conferred Kirti Chakra on Maj. Pradeep Tathawade posthumously. It is second highest gallantry award in peacetime, equivalent of Maha Vir Chakra.

It was an uneasy night for everyone. As the CO, I kept waiting to hear reports of a contact, and Pradeep kept hoping to get some intelligence on movement of terrorists, while the soldiers in the teams deployed in the large area of mountainside kept their eyes and ears peeled for any suspicious movement. The terrorists too must be spending a sleepless night. But where?

10

An Eternal Stamp of Bravery
The Vir Chakra

Terrorists always attempted to infiltrate across the LoC using the cover of nallahs, forests and broken terrain. The Pakistan Army would often resort to unprovoked firing across the LoC to distract the Indian Army and keep their head down while such infiltration attempts were made. Despite their best attempts however, most infiltration attempts would be foiled either at the LoC or eliminated in encounters inside the LoC. Frustrated with this, the Pakistan Army started adopting a new tactic in 1999–2000. They started launching Border Action Teams (BATs) to cause casualties among soldiers manning frontline posts on the Indian side.

The BATs would attempt to cause casualties and then quickly return across the LoC. That is what made it different from infiltration. Their intention was only to cause casualties among soldiers on our posts. These BATs were made-up of terrorists or of a mix of terrorists and Pak Army soldiers, mostly from their special forces who were also giving vent to their frustration on being evicted by the Indian

Army from Kargil in mid-1999. These BATs sometimes would also mutilate the bodies of our soldiers after killing them. This was truly infuriating. Soldiers anywhere don't descend to such depravity.

In one of our high-altitude posts, the distance between our post and Pakistan's posts was a little under a 100 m. Sometimes their soldiers would shout across and use threatening language and swear words. Our soldiers would reply in kind and also add for good measure, sentences like, 'It seems you are not satisfied by being driven out of Kargil. If you try any misadventures here against our paltan, you do will do so at your peril.' They replied in Urdu and the crudity of the language is lost in translation into English, thankfully.

One day, I received intelligence from the Brigade Intelligence Team (BIT) that there was likely to be a BAT action on a couple of their forward posts on the LoC.

'It's a little strange that they would pick on our battalion, which is at a high altitude and that increases the degree of difficulty for them,' I said to Officer-in-Charge (OC), BIT.

He replied, 'Sir, it is because your unit has caused maximum casualties and damage to the terrorists. Several months ago, also they had targeted your battalion HQ with a stand-off rocket attack from Saluniya Ridge for this very reason. They had left a note on their letterhead under a stone there, threatening more such attacks.' I wistfully recalled that rocket attack wistfully, in which terrorists fired rockets at our Bn HQ, but fortunately, we did not suffer any casualties. A letter left under a rock was a backhanded compliment that said that the attack was retaliation for our bn which had killed maximum terrorists.

'Then let them try, we will be ready for them. If they try to surprise us, they will be the ones who will be surprised,' I replied.

'Sir, we should worry more about posts that are in close proximity of enemy posts.'

There were four such posts where Indian and Pakistani posts were in eyeball-to-eyeball configuration. While all posts had been given a due warning, these four posts were put on a special notice. I personally walked up to all these posts and spent a day at each of them to gauge the risk and response myself. At every place I got a similar response from the soldiers, 'Saab *ji aane doh* (let them come), if they dare to come here they will not go back alive, we assure you.'

I felt overwhelmed by their bravery and said a silent prayer of thanks for being part of such a valiant battalion that had such brave troops, who had proved their mettle on every occasion.

During my stay on posts, I shortlisted two posts on which such action was more likely. One, from where our soldiers had launched a raid on the launch pad at the LoC and eliminated five terrorists, and the second at another high-altitude post which I mentioned above. Any post above the altitude of 9,000 feet is classified as high altitude. It increases the degree of difficulty to operate and live on, because of shortage of oxygen. The fatigue factor is also greater. However, the enemy soldiers were being aggressive and belligerent in their firing across the LoC ever since there had been a change of units on the Pakistan side.

I reported this to the Brigade Commander who asked OC BIT to try and confirm intelligence regarding the possibility of BAT action. Meanwhile I ordered an enhanced vigil and aggressive dominance on these posts. Any gaps in manpower and weapons were made up on priority. My soldiers were combat ready and in a combative mood.

One day, Maj. Himanshu Sawant, the Company Commander under whom this high-altitude post was, reported to me that he thought that the enemy seemed to be up to some mischief on the post opposite his. He had seen them strengthening their defences, obstacles and minefields. This was at the high-altitude post shortlisted by them as a likely target.

'Sir, it will be better if we meet at the post so I can brief you in detail.' Though a grammatical paradox, 'briefing in detail' is commonly used phrase in the army. It is also very expressive.

'Very well, I will be there tomorrow,' I replied, smiling at the choice of words. 'I will also ask Maj. Manoj Deshpande and Hav. Chunni Lal from the neighbouring company post to come over so that we can have a brainstorming with more combat-experienced minds.'

The next morning, I set off early. It took an hour-long drive to reach the road-head and a further four-hour walk to reach the post. Deshpande and Chunni, being closer, had reached much earlier. Sawant had reached there from his Charlie Company HQ the previous day itself. Subedar Sat Paul, VrC was the post commander. He was a gallantry medal winner at the Siachen Glacier.

'Jai Durge, Sir,' Sat Paul greeted me with a smile.

'How are you Sat Paul?' I inquired with a lot of warmth. As a Major, I had commanded Charlie Company, and Sat Paul was an NCO then. 'How's the morale of the boys?'

'Always sky-high, Sir,' said Sat Paul. 'It is your company after all.'

'Good, now get me Charlie Company special chai-pakoda, since you've made me walk four hours for it.' I slipped into an easy banter.

'We are looking forward to it, Sir, this is your company.' As if any reminder was needed.

I then met the officers and was happy to see Chunni there as well.

'All well in your company?' I asked Manoj and Chunni.

'All good, Sir,' replied Manoj.

'I'm sure you all have talked about it already, but brief me again.' I said to Himanshu.

'Sir,' he replied, 'I'll let Sat Paul Saab give you a gist of activities first, as he reported to me.'

'Okay, go on,' I said.

Sat Paul cleared his throat and said, 'Sir, for the past few days we're noticing a lot of unusual activities on the enemy post opposite us. Since it is less than a 100 m away, we can observe a lot of their activities, despite their best attempts to hide these.'

'Tell me in detail,' I said, sipping my tea with relish.

'Sir, we see heightened activity of defence maintenance and sprucing up of obstacle system. At night, we have heard sounds of digging and driving iron pickets in the ground that leads me to believe that they may be placing additional mines as well,' he paused for breath and continued, 'There is also an increase in administrative movement of troops and patrols from the post. Several officers have visited the post, including their CO, a few days ago. We reported that to battalion HQ in the daily situation report also.'

'Yes, just like my visit here will be reported in their sitrep this evening,' I said with a smile and they all smiled too.

'There is another change in pattern, Sir,' said Sat Paul, 'Nowadays their sentry does not shout across at all. Earlier they used to shout across frequently, even if it was challenging us or just plain being rude. But nowadays, nothing at all. Not even when provoked. It is as if they have received instructions not to exchange a word at all.'

The troops become very good at such assessments while living constantly on the LoC. They are able to judge the mood or environment of the other side. It is almost like reading the body language equivalent of the adversary, because of proximity and study of habits.

Himanshu added, 'Sir, it is as if they are planning something, and a careless remark should not give the game away.'

'What is your sense?', I asked Manoj.

'Sir, Himanshu and I have spoken about it, and I think they might be planning a BAT action on this post,' Manoj replied.

'So, we must thicken our defences,' I said. 'I'll send you some reinforcements, both men as well as weapon systems.'

'Anything to add?', I turned towards Chunni. I always respected battle experience and the wisdom of NCOs. Some of them came up with earthy out of box ideas and Chunni did not disappoint.

He replied with deliberation, 'Why wait for him to come to us? Why can't we pre-empt his plans?'

'What do you have in mind?'

I well understood what he meant, and was myself so inclined, but I preferred that the junior leaders came up with innovative ideas and the plan and I would only nudge them along with suggestions for improvements. This way, they would have ownership of the plan and feel more responsible to execute it.

'Sir, we could aggressively lay ambushes ahead of our post on the likely approaches. That is sure to take them by surprise,' replied Chunni.

'Yes, Sir. They normally expect us to lay ambushes only in the area between the posts to counter infiltration,' said Manoj.

'Good idea,' I complimented, 'but we will have to negotiate minefields. I know there are safe lanes, but we will have to exercise utmost caution.'

'True, Sir,' said Sat Paul. 'But my boys are familiar with safe lanes, not only in our minefields, but also that of the enemy post. We have seen their movements in their minefields at night using night vision devices.'

'Still, it will be risky,' I cautioned.

'Sir, it is a risk worth taking. Otherwise, BAT actions usually cause a few casualties and withdraw before we can react fully. That is what has happened in other battalions,' said Maj. Himanshu. 'This way we will be able to turn the tables and cause casualties on them.'

I was happy that my boys were suggesting to me exactly what I would have them do. This is called aggressive defence. High risk, high gain. Just like I have been fond of saying often, 'counter terrorist operations are like playing chess with live bullets.' Aloud I said, 'However, we cannot reduce the strength manning the post. So, I'll have to send extra men from other posts. We will get some experienced hands to ensure success. Remember it may not result in any operation on the first night itself, you'll have to send these ambushes for a few nights, starting tonight. Reinforcements will come by this evening. I want two teams to lay aggressive ambushes. Manoj and Himanshu will lead one team each. I'm sure Manoj, you'll want Chunni with you,' I smiled.

'I'll let you organize your teams. But remember to seize any fleeing opportunity you get. That is what makes the difference between successful and very successful. Best of luck. Happy hunting.'

The Knock-Out Punch

Men started arriving from other companies that evening. There were three additional sections, all comprising seasoned soldiers, veterans of many operations in the LoC and in the hinterland. Some of them had participated in the raid on the launch pad and Hav. Chunni Lal was particularly happy to see Rfn Zalam Singh, as they both were together in that operation. He was fearless and a very reassuring fellow to have with you in a tricky situation.

Once they had all had a cup of tea and settled in, Manoj and Himanshu briefed them about the impending task in detail. They stressed on the fact that after leaving their own bunkers, there should be no talking and no noise to maintain surprise. Therefore, it was important that all contingencies were discussed in advance.

After that Sat Paul and Chunni personally checked their weapons and equipment. It was important that the weapons fired smoothly and the equipment did not make any noise in such close proximity of the enemy post.

They all ate their dinner early and about one hour after last light, left their defences to lay ambushes ahead. Two minefield-safe lanes were used. Prem Lal was leading Himanshu's column and Chunni Lal was leading Manoj's column. It is a coincidence that they both belonged to Doda District. They moved in crouch position through the crawl trench. A crawl trench is dug or created between bunkers, so that soldiers can move from one bunker to another without being detected by the enemy. Then they crawled through the safe lanes through own minefield. They moved on their forearms and knees to escape detection. They reached the edge of their minefield and found a suitable place to lay ambushes from where they could observe the enemy post and approaches leading to their post.

Chunni whispered to Manoj, 'Sir, why don't we just go ahead and do a stand-off firing on their post?'

They were barely 40 m to 50 m from the enemy post.

Manoj smiled at Chunni's josh. 'We will not achieve much when they are in their bunkers. Let's wait for them to collect to try and launch a raid on our post as expected, then we will get them in the open. That way we can cause more damage.'

Chunni saw the sense of that. They waited patiently. Waiting in an ambush is one of the most difficult operations. You cannot move much, not make a noise, not even cough. Any sound can alert the enemy, and then you become sitting ducks.

In the other column Himanshu was on one side and Sat Paul on the other side of the ambush. They were on a steep slope and could observe the enemy bunkers from a distance of 50 m or so. They lay motionless without making any sound. Suddenly, someone in the middle shifted his position and a dry twig snapped. The sound it made sounded too loud because of the stillness around. But nothing happened. You get an exaggerated sense of caution in you when you are in close proximity of the enemy.

After a while, Sat Paul felt the urge to cough. He was trying to control it. He wished he had packed some Vicks or Strepsils lozenges in his backpack. However, he did not dare cough. A human cough would certainly give away the surprise. He frantically looked around, then he plucked some grass and started chewing on it. The saliva it produced calmed the irritation in his throat somewhat and the urge to cough subsided. Phew! His presence of mind saved the day.

They laid the ambush, with a reserve team poised about 20 m behind both these teams. They all remained motionless for the better part of the night. Manoj's ambush was closer to the first bunker of the enemy. A couple of times Chunni observed the enemy sentry moving about looking in their direction, but obviously oblivious of them. He nudged Manoj and pointed it out to him. A couple of other soldiers also observed the movement. They all froze. It was an unnerving feeling. It seemed to them that their presence had been discovered. Tense times.

However, the night passed without any incident. At around 0400 hours in the morning, Manoj signalled and they all started crawling out of their position one by one, back to their post. He also whispered the agreed code word 'Jai Durge' to Himanshu on the radio set. Their team also did likewise. The withdrawal had to be equally quiet, lest they give away surprise and invite enemy firing.

After reaching their posts, they all picked up mugs of steaming hot tea and pakoras from the cookhouse and sat in a huddle for a quick debrief.

'What a waste!', said Sat Paul.

'Not at all, Sir,' said Chunni, 'I think it was a good rehearsal. We also observed their sentry a few times and have a good idea where they are likely to get together to launch a raid on our post. I think it was most useful.'

'We could not see anything,' said Sat Paul, 'We were perched on a steep slope."

Himanshu said, 'That itself is good to know. Now we know what to expect. We will have to focus on listening drills to detect their approach, since we can't observe them till they are very close.

Manoj sipped his tea, smiled and said, 'The inter se distance is only 40 to 50 m. Everything is close if we have to rush them. Remember, we must seize the initiative. They should be bewildered. Only then we can succeed in our mission without any casualties and withdraw.'

They all retired to their bunkers for a well-earned rest. Since the post was his company post. Himanshu called me up on a field telephone and reported the whole episode. I had many queries, and he answered all, providing details.

At last I said, 'Himanshu, the intelligence is confirmed. They will carry out a raid on our post in a day or two. Terrorists don't really use that high-altitude area for infiltration. Thus, the intel also says that it is likely be launched by the regular troops deployed opposite.'

'Don't worry, Sir, they won't surprise us. On the contrary, they are in for a surprise,' replied Himanshu.

'Best of luck. I will also join you at the post by this evening,' I said before disconnecting.

Himanshu smiled. They all knew that their CO could not resist being in action or close to where the action was. This norm of senior officers remaining with the troops in action had an operational logic to it. If the CO was present on the site, he did not have to depend on progress reports on the radio or through his staff officers. If he knew the situation in real time, he could coordinate any other relevant activity with other sub units, like asking for supporting fire from a neighbouring locality or heavier weapons, or co-ordinate casualty evacuation by chopper if required, movement of reinforcement if needed, and so on. The CO is also at hand, if any quick decisions are required, and his presence at post has a morale boosting effect.

I arrived on the post well before last light. I addressed the boys in a low voice before they went for dinner. 'It is good that you had a full dress rehearsal last night. Now you all are fully prepared, aren't you?'

'Yes, Sir!' was the muted but vehement response.

The teams left at about 2100 hours. It was a clear night. I would have preferred it to be cloudy, so that visibility was restricted and even sound carried less. But everything else was set. They not only knew their respective teams, they also knew the order of march. Havildar Chunni and Hav. Prem were in lead. Subedar Sat Paul and a few others were carrying throat drops. They repeated the same motions as previous night and were soon deployed in their ambush sites, with their sights trained intently on enemy movement. After all, the enemy was planning to come and kill them. It was the survival of the fittest. Kill or be killed. There are no runners-up in battle. Those who don't win, often end up dead. Unlike the movies, survival in battle is matter of fact and to the point. There is no grandstanding. There is simply no time for it.

Chunni had crawled around to his left and right to ensure that the inter se distance between our soldiers was the way it should be. Neither bunching up, nor farther than a whisper range away. The soldiers felt reassured when a seasoned veteran and a gallantry medal winner like Chunni Lal moved among them in the battlefield. Similarly, Sat Paul did the same on the other team to similar effect.

A little after 2200 hours, Chunni observed some movement from the enemy post. He drew Manoj's attention to it. Manoj signalled that he had already seen it. They signalled everyone to observe ahead. They could make out four soldiers crouching forward, ahead of their post. They came up to a clearing and took lying position on all four corners.

Chunni felt excited. If they were securing an area, it should be for other soldiers to follow, once they were assured that all was clear. Manoj was using night-vision goggles to observe the area ahead. Those days the Army had infrared-based night vision devices, not thermal imagery-based ones. Though not as good, they still provided enough clarity to make out the movements at such close range. It was a clear night, unfortunately. 'Unfortunately', because a cloudy night would hide their movements from the enemy. However, it would also hide the enemy's movements from them.

Now, they could make out more soldiers crouching their way forward. Chunni estimated that ten men had deployed in the area. Someone looked over his shoulders and said something. They could not make out what was said, it seemed like a whispered order. Chunni whispered to Manoj, 'We should charge at them with our weapons firing.'

Chunni was always impatient to get into action. Manoj signalled him to wait, maybe more men would join, but it couldn't be delayed much. Manoj was right, two more soldiers joined carrying something.

Manoj put his mouth near Chunni's ear and whispered, 'We should wait till they make a move. They will present a bigger target and be a bit unbalanced then. Right now, they are secure.' Chunni's heart was beating wildly in anticipation of imminent action.

The enemy soldiers did not make any move for quite some time. It was as though they were waiting for a go ahead or for another party to reach at another point. Chunni felt they could be building up at two places or approaches. Launching two separate approaches is a military tactic that serves three purposes. It divides the enemy's attention, the two thrusts can support each other and finally, if one approach gets stalled, the other can get the work done.

It was a macabre situation. Both sides were waiting, albeit for different reasons. The Indian side was at an advantage, in that they knew the presence of the adversary, whereas the adversary did not know of their presence. Manoj was fully conscious that they had to capitalize on this advantage. On his signal, he, Chunni and another buddy pair started crawling cautiously and very slowly towards the left. The rest would provide covering fire from the present position. This contingency had been planned for and rehearsed, as had been many others. They were careful not to make any sound. The sky was partly clear, but there was no moon yet.

Meanwhile, they could hear the Pakistan soldiers talking in low voices, as if last minute confirmations were being ascertained. As if on an order that our soldiers could not hear, they cocked their weapons. The simple act of cocking of weapons, something all soldiers were used to all their lives, suddenly sounded very loud in the stillness of the night. Some of the soldiers in the ambush were startled.

Then the enemy soldiers got up and slowly started moving forward. They were walking in a crouch with their weapons pointed to the front, ready to fire.

Chunni tensed, ready to fire. He also realized that his Company Commander was right, they presented a more vulnerable target now while moving, especially from a flank.

Suddenly, Manoj fired a burst from his AK Rifle at the Pak soldiers who were advancing to attack our post. That was the signal. Chunni felt a rush of adrenaline course through his body as he also opened fire. So did everyone else. Over the noise of gunfire, they heard shouts from the enemy soldiers. Must be exclamations of disbelief or pain or both. Recovering from the shock, a couple of them fired back, but their firing was haywire, driven by panic and not aimed.

However, Manoj, Chunni and their two comrades had already dropped to the ground. The others left behind at the ambush site had started firing a couple of seconds later. The enemy's attention was divided in two directions.

Soon there was a heavy barrage of machine gunfire from the bunkers at the Pakistan post. Manoj, Chunni and others slid down the slope to the left. Since they were on a spine on the ridge, by doing so they could save themselves from flat trajectory of the bullets of machine guns. The real trouble would start when the Pakistani soldiers started firing mortars and artillery.

As had been pre-decided, our own post also opened heavy fire on the Pakistan post in retaliation. The ambush party had also slid down towards the right, and thus were safe from this exchange of fire between posts. Chunni took out a hand grenade from his pouch. After the safety pin is pulled out, the grenade explodes in four seconds. Since the enemy was out in the open, he pulled out the pin and released the safety lever in his hand itself.

The four-second-count had begun. He paused for two seconds and then lobbed the grenade on the enemy soldiers in a high arc. Since two seconds had already elapsed, the grenade could not land on the ground. It exploded in the air itself over the Pakistani soldiers. This is called an air burst and causes more casualties than a grenade that explodes on the ground, since some of the impact is absorbed by the ground itself. It is risky and not every soldier can do it, especially under battlefield conditions. But Chunni was experienced, with regard to this and his team was safe behind the rise of the ridgeline.

Meanwhile, the moment firing started Himanshu's party crawled towards the enemy post to get a better view so that they could fire effectively from a different direction. Since they were on a steep slope, a couple of soldiers lost their footing and slid down the re-entrant. The lead man, Prem Lal was one of them. The enemy had laid mines in the re-entrant, as they heard a couple of explosions. Two mines had been activated by Prem Lal sliding over them. He was wounded in his foot and hip and was groaning. Sat Paul detached two men to tend to him and the other soldier who had slid down. The rest of them, led by Himanshu, reached the edge from where they started firing at the post. Now Pakistan's BAT was caught in a cross-fire from three directions.

After a few minutes of intense firing, there was a perceptible slowdown in firing from the Pakistani post.

'They will try to evacuate their wounded soldiers back into the safety of the post.' Manoj said.

'Then we must crawl forward and get a couple of their bodies and take them away,' replied Chunni.

'Why?'

'Sir, Pakistan always claims that it is the "freedom fighters" who launch such actions. We will be able to show their duplicity in launching BAT action on our post by regular soldiers.'

That made perfect sense.

So Chunni crawled back and got more soldiers from their ambush team and together they crawled forward towards where they had shot the enemy soldiers who were ready to attack their post. There was firing all around. Our post was firing, Himanshu's team was firing. Two of the neighbouring posts from both sides were firing at each other. The LoC had got totally activated. Several flares had also been fired by the Pakistan side to spot the enemy. It seemed chaotic all around.

Manoj was reminded of a sentence that he had read long ago, '... And central peace subsisting at the heart of endless agitation.'[16] That's how he and Chunni felt. They also felt a rush of adrenaline as they rushed forward, saw the enemy soldiers lying dead, and carried three bodies down the slope before their comrades from the post could get to them. Major Manoj quickly radioed for mortar fire on Pakistan posts to cover their withdrawal.

I ordered the mortars to start giving covering fire and soon mortars started shelling Pakistan posts. Under the cover of mortar shelling, it was imperative to withdraw now, before enemy artillery shelling started. Our soldiers got up and started withdrawing. They ran in crouch position for a few metres and got into a deep crawl trench in their own minefield, which had been prepared for the purpose of this withdrawal. Chunni kept encouraging his men to hurry, carrying three dead soldiers as they were. Havildar Joginder, who was bringing up the rear, was another very joshila junior leader who kept up the morale of the boys by constantly encouraging words.

Meanwhile, their move was also effectively covered by Himanshu's team who continued to engage the attention and firing of the enemy post.

This is the sense of duty and feeling of reassurance in the army. Despite having lost two soldiers, Himanshu's team kept covering the withdrawal of Manoj's team, as per the assigned task. Mission always comes first. Their route of withdrawal was different and safe from flat trajectory weapons, but they would also be exposed in the open when the enemy started shelling by mortars and artillery. Speed was of essence. As soon as their last soldier, Joginder, jumped into the crawl trench in our own minefield, Manoj ordered the withdrawal of Himanshu's team as well. A deep crawl trench offers a fair degree of protection against shelling as well, unless a shell lands inside the trench itself. That would be pure bad luck.

After a while when they all reached their post, they all took stock of the situation before reporting to me. I had been closely monitoring the activities from the post and keeping the higher HQ informed. This is an important role a CO plays in such operations, to interface between stakeholders, so that those participating in operations are left free to carry out the operations. I also coordinated firing from other posts and the mortar shelling, so that the soldiers in the operations didn't have to look over their shoulders for anything.

The operation was a great success. The soldiers had thwarted a BAT action on their post by launching a pre-emptive spoiling attack on them. They had brought back bodies of three enemy soldiers, but sadly we had also lost two soldiers. It is an occupational hazard. But these two soldiers were heroes. In all likelihood there would have been several casualties, had the enemy been successful in launching the BAT action on their post.

An interesting bit of news lightened up the mood somewhat. Havildar Joginder's trouser legs had two bullet holes behind his thigh. Apparently, a bullet had gone through his trouser leg without him even coming to know of it! Phew! That was a close shave. God works in mysterious ways. He had been rewarded for all his josh and for risking remaining exposed in the open till all the soldiers of his section were safely inside the crawl trench.

Later, when they all had reached their post, Himanshu said he had felt a searing, burning sensation under his foot while withdrawing to our own post. When they examined his boots, they saw that the sole of the right boot had a slight furrow cut below it. it could have been caused by a bullet or a shrapnel. They'd nearly had two more casualties.

The bodies of the dead Pakistani soldiers were handed over to the Pakistan Army at a flag meeting at Suchetgarh near Jammu as proof that BAT actions were also being done by regular soldiers. It was learnt through intelligence reports later that the enemy had suffered fourteen casualties. Major Manoj and Hav. Chunni Lal were awarded a Vir Chakra each, the nation's third-highest gallantry medal, and Hav. Joginder was awarded the Sena Medal, which is next award in the pecking order.

Several days later Defence Minister George Fernandes visited the Division HQ and addressed the troops. Having learnt of the gallant action of my battalion, he expressed a desire to visit my paltan and compliment the brave boys himself. It was a brief visit. He landed at our HQ helipad by a chopper. I was amazed to see him dressed so simply in a kurta-pyjama. He came across as a very humble man.

He was accompanied by the top brass. However, I drove him from the helipad to my base in my gypsy. During the drive he said, 'I have been told what a great job your battalion has been doing in this area, against the enemy as well against the terrorists. Well done.'

I said, 'Sir, I am fortunate to command such brave soldiers. They know no fear.'

At the base, he addressed all the soldiers present at a special Sainik Sammelan. He began by paying homage to Hav. Prem Lal and Rfn

Gopal Dass. He then complimented the boys for their bravery. The boys felt highly motivated by the visit of the Defence Minister, accompanied by the Army Commander, the Corps Commander, the Division Commander and the Brigade Commander. It is rare, if not unprecedented to have such a high profile visit at the battalion level. He met some of those who had participated in the operation. I began introducing the boys in the line-up. When he came in front of Hav. Chunni Lal, I pointed out, 'Sir, he is one of the bravest soldiers of the Indian Army. Not only has he participated in several operations here in the last two years, but he was awarded a Sena Medal in the highest attack in the world at the Siachen Glacier over a decade ago.'

The Defence Minister threw a salute and said, '*Sara desh aapki bahaduri ko* salute *karta hai*.' (The entire nation salutes your bravery). Thank you for your service.'

Chunni simply said, 'Jai Hind, Sir, I just did my duty.'

'It was the survival of the fittest. Kill or be killed. There are no runners-up in battle. Those who don't win, often end up dead. Unlike the movies, survival in battle is matter of fact and to the point. There is no grandstanding. There is simply no time for it.'

11

Voh Dekh Raha Hai

A<small>FTER A SUCCESSFUL</small> term of duty in Poonch, Hav. Chunni Lal was posted to Officers Training Academy (OTA) at Kamptee in Maharashtra, as an instructor in 2001. This academy trains the Associated NCC Officers, called ANOs for short. They are basically school or college teachers who conduct NCC (National Cadet Corps) parades and training activities. The academy also conducts orientation training for Army JCOs and NCOs, when they are posted to NCC units as permanent staff.

Chunni was obviously posted there as a trainer because of a rare combination of military skills as a Weapons Instructor, and his motivational abilities as a double gallantry medal winner. The irony was that the Army used 7.62 mm self-loading rifles, whereas the NCC cadets are trained on .22 rifles. Hence, Chunni had to learn first from other instructors, as they all do. But he was a fast learner, and the basics are the same anyway.

Kamptee is the centre point of India, 14 km from Nagpur. It has numerous old barracks from the British days and lore has it that the British officers were initially brought here to Central India for orientation training to enable them to serve in Royal Indian Army.

As always, Chunni Lal was very good at his work. He had a great amount of professional pride, whether it was on the battlefield or in the training area or on the Parade ground. He was always correctly turned out, wore his medals with pride, was impeccable in his behaviour with staff and students alike, and also acutely conscious of the fact that the trainees were essentially teachers and professors. He gave them due respect and they in turn, adored him. He was so down to earth and humble. He was often asked about his combat experience, 'Please tell us how you won these medals?' to which his responses were a lesson in humility. He would always say, 'I just did my duty.'

During his stay there, he brought his family to live with him. It was the only station where his family joined him. He enjoyed spending his free time with his children, especially his youngest daughter who was just a couple of years old. A soldier misses the beautiful experience of the growing up of his child, Chunni was getting a small feel of it.

'Now I realize what I have missed so far in life,' he told his wife wistfully. 'What we all soldiers miss when we stay and spend time in operational areas, where families are not permitted.'

It was during his stay at OTA Kamptee, that Hav. Chunni Lal was invited to the investiture ceremony at the Rashtrapati Bhawan, where he was awarded the Vir Chakra formally. It was a simple, but elegant ceremony. Major Manoj Deshpande was also there. He came down from the Indian Military Academy (IMA), his alma mater, where he was posted now an instructor. He was an inspiration to the officer cadets, just as Hav. Chunni Lal was an inspirational figure in OTA.

Their meeting in Delhi brought joy to their hearts. 'How have you been Chunni? So good to see you again,' said Manoj.

'Sir, I'm fine. How are you? Good to meet you in a civilized place,' smiled Chunni, as they hugged.

They had met at the rehearsal one day prior to the investiture ceremony. Thereafter, they went to a hotel for a celebratory drink together. They swapped stories of old times. It is then that Manoj realized the import of Chunni's words about meeting at a civilized place. They were used to being together in mountains and jungles also, when bullets were flying around.

Chunni said, 'Sir, today you will have to allow me to pay for the drink. The treat is on me.'

In the army, tradition has it that the senior pays on such occasions. But the intense look on Chunni's face forbade Manoj to refuse his offer. It showed that Chunni's character was so different. He had firm conviction and a supreme self-confidence about him. This is what the younger generation call swag.

The next day, they received their Vir Chakra medals from President Abul Kalam, together. Both of them felt happy that not only were they both together during the operation but they both were also awarded their medals together. It made their bond stronger.

When some senior officers congratulated him after the ceremony and said 'Well done', he simply said, 'Sir, I just did my duty.'

Back at OTA, Maj. Sean O'Brien organized a function to felicitate Hav. Chunni Lal. Yes, he was the same Sean from his battalion and both happened to be posted to OTA together. The hall was full of ANOs, NCC cadets, instructors and staff officers.

During the informal interaction that followed, one cadet asked Hav. Chunni Lal, 'Sir, how did you feel during the operation?'

'I did not feel anything,' was the reply.

'You did not feel anything while killing the enemy or terrorists?'

'You don't feel any compunctions when you are in a "kill or be killed" situation. When one of us has to die, I would rather it be the enemy soldiers or the terrorists.'

He would generally cap all discussions by saying, 'I did my duty.'

There lies the bittersweet fact of an Army soldier's ethos. A soldier also kills, but that is his duty.

At OTA, Kamptee, the Parade ground was named after him, after he made the supreme sacrifice in north Kashmir, and his bust was installed there. All trainees since then pay respect to the great hero, who was once instructor here. They pay their respects not only as a part of drill and practice, but also as veneration to the bravest Indian soldier.

They say, '*Voh dekh raha hai.*'

He is looking. He is watching over us.

He still inspires!

'You don't feel any compunctions when you are in a "kill or be killed" situation. When one of us has to die, I would rather it be the enemy soldiers or the terrorist.' 'There lies the bittersweet fact of an Army soldier's ethos. A soldier also kills, but that is his duty.'

12

Global Peacekeeping Round II
Sudan and Onwards

SUDAN IS A large country in Africa and has a rich culture. It was a French, and later a British colony till it was granted independence in 1956. As in the case of various other British-ruled colonies, their governance in Sudan was regulatory with few developmental programmes. Sadly, even after independence the country could not reap the fruits of development due to the faulty policies of its leaders.

Prior to being under French and then British rule, the country was ruled by Muslims who came from Arab countries and settled down in the Northern part of Sudan. The cultural differences of its population divided the country into two distinct parts. The north was inhabited by the ruling clan (Muslims; now the ruling party), and was adequately developed; while the south had animists, a few Christians and some Muslims, was totally underdeveloped and over the years was neglected by the government.[17]

The people in the southern part of the country took up arms to get their autonomy and legitimate revenue for development of the area. Dr Johan Grange (who later died in a helicopter crash) organized the South Sudanese Peoples Liberation Army (SPLA for short) and a political wing, the South Sudanese Liberation Movement (SPLM). The Sudanese Armed Forces (SAF) kept this secessionist movement under control.

Initially, not much progress could be made by southern Sudan to get its rights, The Sudanese government would not easily agree to their demands because southern Sudan was (and is) very rich in natural resources such as minerals and crude oil.

Seeing the momentum of the SPLA and fearing interference by the international community, the Sudanese government (headquartered in the north) quickly concluded a number of crude oil contracts with China for a period of fifteen years. Diplomatic relations between Sudan and the United States (US) were not very cordial as the former apprehended that the movement to create the separate nation of South Sudan was being assisted by the US.

The movement of SPLA caught up with the help of some of neighbouring African countries, and at places the SPLA pushed back the SAF within southern Sudan and established its own strongholds. Local support, in any case, was with the SPLA. These activities of the SPLA and the SPLM, coupled with diplomatic pressure, forced the Sudanese government to enter into an agreement with representatives of southern Sudan, which paved the way for establishment of the UN Mission in Sudan.

The United Nations Mission in Sudan (UNMIS) was established in 2005. It was an extremely challenging environment for the UN, in which to establish the mission. It faced a lot of problems at the initial stages due to existing complexities, being an underdeveloped country with decades-old ongoing turmoil, lawlessness, poor governance and lack of cooperation from the people.

The Indian government contributed troops in accordance with the UN's mandate as a part of UNMIS, and established its mission in Sudan in 2005. A team of Indian officers visited Khartoum, the capital city of Sudan. The initial visits and analysis of the tasks revealed that establishing the Indian mission in the south of the country was a very challenging assignment, because the area was devoid of any local resources, was beset by poor governance, and was dealing with the conflict in full swing. The mission thus was a great administrative and operational challenge and needed detailed planning on each aspect for meticulous execution.

The Sector[18] was headed by Col Bharat Singh Shekhawat, CO of 8 JAKLI (Siachen), my battalion. Havildar Chunni Lal, VrC, SM, from Bravo Company was part of the mission. By now, he had an established reputation of being brave, having great initiative, and ability to lead from the front. Visualizing the complexities of the Mission, the CO selected Hav. Chunni Lal to be part of his Core Team and Quick Response Team. He, therefore, accompanied the CO in the Advance Group that landed at Al Obeid, far away from Conflict Zone. There they regrouped themselves and carried out orientation training before moving to Mission area, Malakal.

The makeshift Sector HQ was being run by Military Observers at Malakal. The CO, Col Bharat Shekhawat had to go there to update himself and take charge and then get the Advance Group into the Mission area. The CO decided to take his buddy and Chunni along with him. They landed at Malakal and Chunni was indispensable for the next few days. He was the CO's security guard, one-man protection, and adviser. Fortunately, they had done some language training in Sudanese, and Hav. Chunni Lal always carried his notes, with help of which he would communicate with locals.

They had to find a suitable site for camping for their unit, so they had to move around. The area was infested with snakes and even had unmarked mines. Once while walking, the CO almost bumped into a deadly snake in the middle of the road. Havildar Chunni had a hawk's eye and was so vigilant that he not only shouted out a warning to the CO but also jumped in front of the CO to prevent the snake from biting him. While moving around for reconnaissance on the banks of Nile River or in open ground, many a time he would at a first observe the area well, appreciate and warn the CO to say, 'Saab ye area mined *lagta hai*' (Sir, this area seems to be mined). His gut feeling always turned out to be true. No wonder then, that every CO wanted Hav. Chunni Lal to be with him.

The role of the UN Peacekeeping mission was primarily mediation. They were not to fight with the either party except in self-defence. To perform their job, they had to win the hearts and minds of people. With vast experience of fighting insurgency, Hav. Chunni Lal formed part of CO's Core Group to identify local issues which could be addressed quickly and be a meaningful welfare measure. He was instrumental in establishing different sites for the unit on ground, moving stores in barges on the Nile.

Malakal and the areas around had it frequent fire incidents since the houses there were made of grass and mud. Havildar Chunni was often the lead member in reaching out to extinguish fires in town. During one of the nights, he bravely moved out with just one water bowser and a few soldiers to extinguish a major fire in the town, thus saving lives and property. The next very day the Governor of Malakal and other civilian dignitaries complimented the CO and honoured Hav. Chunni Lal and his team. This was a first step wherein the battalion established a close contact and trust with the locals.

Akobo, a small town situated along the Ethiopian border witnessed tribal clashes in April 2006 that resulted in the killing of eleven persons and left twenty-three injured. Braving inhospitable weather, a team was despatched under Maj. Devender Singh to deploy at Akobo. Havildar Chunni was the NCO in charge of the lead section. The boys landed at a makeshift helipad in the middle of the crisis situation and carried out effective domination for about a week, to ensure peace with meagre resources, till the situation improved and more reinforcements could be pushed in. Akobo is only one such example. The battalion ensured peace at sixteen such flash-points, and every officer wanted Hav. Chunni Lal to be a part of his team. He exhibited such bravery and commitment and was absolutely fearless. He was a role model, not only to his comrades, but to the international staff as well.

There was a sore point as far as the battalion's assigned mission was concerned. Self-styled SPLA General, Tangue held total sway over the Fam Al Zeraf area. There was terror in the area. He refused to allow deployment of Military Observers. The UNMIS had to establish a footprint there to start a dialogue with Gen. Tangue to put the peace programme into effect. The CO sent several messages to meet him, but he declined. The CO ordered the Military Observers of another country to venture out, but they appeared very reluctant. As a last resort, Col Shekhawat discussed with a couple of his officers, the possibility of forcibly landing in the area of this warlord on a chopper. They were all of the opinion that the rebels would fire at the helicopter and not allow it to land.

When Hav. Chunni Lal learnt of this, he approached the CO. 'Sir,' he said, 'we must establish contact with Gen Tangue, as this is an unfulfilled part of our mission.'

'You are right, Chunni, but it seems he does not want any contact with us, and he is in total control.'

'Sir, how about going there by helicopter, I will accompany you. With your negotiating skills, you will be able work out something with him.'

'I was of the same opinion, but I have been advised that it may not be safe, his men will open fire on the chopper. That could create a bigger international incident.'

'Not if the helipad is secured first,' replied Chunni.

'How?' asked the CO, although in a flash he guessed what the answer was going to be.

'Sir, let me go and secure the helipad area first. We will sanitize the area and ensure no rebels are present during the landing of your chopper. Their fight is not with us. They will not want to invite a bigger backlash.'

The CO asked, 'How will you go?'

Chunni replied, 'We will take a boat patrol on the Nile.'

It was an audacious plan. So audacious that it could just work.

Relieved to find a way out of this impasse, the CO gave the go-ahead.

Chunni was always happy to take a plunge into new risky situations. It was as if it gave him a high. In this case, he was right. The river patrol took nearly three hours to cover the over 100 km distance. They did not encounter anyone at the helipad. On Hav. Chunni Lal's communication, Col Shekhawat took off in a MI 17 helicopter, which had been requisitioned for the purpose in advance and had been awaiting clearance from Chunni's team. It was a short, twenty-minute flight. On reaching the site, initially, the pilots were a little unsure. But when they all saw the thumbs up and the wave by Hav. Chunni Lal, they were reassured. They landed safely.

They made contact with Gen Tangue, and Col Shekhawat persuaded him to work for peace. The Colonel also kept his word and negotiated with Government of southern Sudan and sent the General to Khartoum, thus paving the way for peace in the area. Havildar Chunni's contribution was praiseworthy.

The Malakal Crisis

There was large-scale violence in Malakal during the last few days of the year, from 27 November to 5 December 2006, to be precise. During these eight days there was outright conflict between the troops of the SPLA and the SAF for commissionership of Fam Al Zeraf. There was widespread violence and high tension in the area. The situation was getting out of control and over 100 persons were killed over first two nights, and 200 injured.

The Indian Battalion had to intervene proactively to put an end to the fighting. Havildar Chunni was detailed to shift international staff out of Malakal. He audaciously led the Quick Reaction Team, passing through both the adversarial forces fighting for control of Malakal Airport and successfully evacuated the civilian staff to a safe zone. Subsequently, Hav. Chunni Lal was also an important member of Area Domination Patrol during the serious fighting.

The Force Commander was an Indian General, Lt Gen J.S. Lidder. He wanted to land at Malakal with the Ceasefire Joint Monitoring Committee (CJMC) members to engage in dialogue with the warring sides. He spoke to the CO on a phone call and the CO explained, 'Sir, there is heavy fighting around Malakal Airport, and it is not possible to land.'

When this continued for a couple of hours, the Force Commander lost his patience and told the CO, 'Thakur Saab, I am taking off, do what you have to. If they shoot me, I will take my chances.'

Major Himanshu Sawant volunteered to brave through the firing from the tanks, to contact one of the SPLA commanders to speak to him, and he took Hav. Chunni Lal with him in his team. They conveyed their CO's message to the SPLA Commander: the Force Commander would be landing soon and if the warring factions did not cease fire for a couple of hours, they would use rocket launchers to blow up their tanks. Although this was an idle threat, as a peacekeeping mission could not use weapons except in self-defence, it worked. There was a ceasefire and the Force Commander and his delegation could land safely, because of that courageous action by Maj. Himanshu's team.

Their arrival and the subsequent negotiations paved the way for lasting peace. Twenty-five officers and men, including Maj. Himanshu and Hav. Chunni Lal were awarded the Force Commander's Commendation Cards and the battalion was awarded the UN Citation for distinguished services rendered.

Havildar Chunni was always happy to take a plunge into new risky situations. It was as if it gave him a high. In this case, he was right.

13

The Last Operation

THE BATTALION RETURNED to India after completing its tenure in Sudan in early 2007, having earned praise from all the dignitaries in their chain of command. It had done the country proud and been awarded the Force Commander's Citation for their exemplary service under the aegis of UN Peacekeeping Force in Sudan, UNMIS.

A Jangi Paltan, the battalion was now deployed in north Kashmir, an area rife with terrorism. Kashmir was still grappling with cross-border terrorism that was being exported by Pakistan. Pakistan and its Inter-Services Intelligence (ISI) not only supported the terrorist groups in J&K, but also sent in terrorists from Pakistan, sometimes even a few radicalized jihadists from other countries like Afghanistan. They infiltrated the LoC, using the broken terrain, which is thickly forested, replete with streams and nallahs. It is mostly covered with pine forests, and has a lot of deodars, 'cheed' and poplar trees as well. During the winters it is covered with snow that makes movement difficult. Especially when coupled with bad weather and poor visibility, it favours the terrorists in sneaking across the LoC.

The Indian Army guards the borders diligently. The major difference to be seen from the battalion's previous Poonch tenure, was that an anti-infiltration fence had been created behind the LoC. This fence is still in use and has different types of sensors affixed on it to help in detection of terrorists. The Indian Army deploys ambushes to block infiltration. Such an ambush is conducted by a group of soldiers, usually eight to ten, who are tactically deployed to guard a likely route of infiltration.

Soldiers like Chunni, who had by now been promoted as Naib Subedar, were very valuable in such operational deployments, owing to their experience on the LoC, in high altitude and in combat, not to mention two tenures in different countries in the UN Peacekeeping Force. Naib Subedar Chunni Lal had seen it all. Having an eye for the ground, locating the right man at the right place in an ambush, opening fire on the terrorists when detected, at the right time—not early, not late—are the key factors, and vital for survival. The terrorist will kill you if you don't kill him first. If you open fire when he is still out of your effective range, he will run away and escape. Therefore, a judicious balance had to be drawn on when to fire.

Kupwara is 85 km north of Srinagar. The route passes through Baramulla and Handwara. The battalion was deployed in Kupwara District on the Shamshabari Mountain Range further to the northwest of Kupwara Town. The Shamshabari Mountain Range runs along the north and northwest side of the Kashmir Valley. To its south is the Jhelum River Valley, and to the north is the Kishanganga River Valley. In this part, the LoC generally runs along Kishenganga River, which is called the Neelam River once it enters Pakistan.

In such deployments, units perform the dual task of guarding the LoC as well as guarding against infiltration. The broad requirements to fulfil these missions are absolutely different from each other. To protect the sovereignty of the LoC, we have to deploy soldiers on dominating heights, so that they can observe large areas all around and also bring down effective fire of long-range weapons on advancing or attacking enemy soldiers.

On the other hand, terrorists use nallahs, re-entrants and thickly wooded areas to infiltrate unnoticed. To prevent this, soldiers have to undertake ambushes in these low-lying areas, and on likely routes. In short, it implies that troops have to be deployed all across the LoC. Thus, every inch of the LoC cannot be manned. The likely routes of infiltration are appreciated and sensors and night vision devices are deployed to get an early warning of attempted infiltration. On discerning such attempts, ambushes are adjusted and re-sited accordingly.

This is what exactly happened on 23 June 2007. The Long-Range Reconnaissance and Observation System (LORROS; a powerful long-range day and night observation system) Detachment deployed at one of the dominating heights observed some of terrorists attempting to infiltrate in the early hours of morning. The Company Commander, Lt Col Sean O'Brien, was informed. He was also officiating as CO of the battalion that day, as the CO had gone to higher HQ on some official business.

Naib Subedar Chunni Lal was the post commander on that post towards which the terrorists were climbing up.

As officiating CO, Lt Col Sean spoke to Nb Sub. Chunni on telephone. Each post is connected by telephone, and radio communication is used as back up.

'Chunni, get ready, some action is coming your way. Are you ready?'

They both went back a long way in the paltan and had been in several combat situations together, with healthy mutual respect.

'You know it, Sir, I'm always more than ready for action,' said Chunni with easy familiarity and with even more enthusiasm, 'and so are my boys.'

They evaluated the situation. Their posts were on top of the Shamshabari Range. The infiltrators had been spotted on our side of the LoC. They had managed to bypass the BSF Outpost located at the valley floor, and were seen briefly moving up the re-entrants and nallahs towards the crest of Shamshabari Range, before they disappeared from view of the night sight.

'They are likely to reach your location by first light, at the crack of dawn,' said Lt Col Sean.

Naib Subedar Chunni felt they would cross the crest an hour or two before first light. 'Their aim will be to cross the Shamshabari Range before first light and merge in the population that resides on the southern slopes,' he said.

The Shamshabari Range has a peculiar dynamic. On the forward slopes there are very few Kashmiris, but more of Machali and Gujjars, who are not as radicalized. Even to the west of this area, the forward slopes have a Pahari majority and to the east in Gurez valley, there is a higher percentage of Gurezi population. That is the reason why terrorists aim to cross the crest of the mountain range well before first light and merge in the villages that are more sympathetic to their cause. And that is also the reason why the anti-infiltration fence has been erected by the Army along the crest line in this part.

Naib Subedar Chunni re-sited his ambush in anticipation. He personally went from man to man, saw their positions, adjusted their positions in order to get best field of view and field of fire. His men found his presence and instructions reassuring and morale boosting. He had been in numerous combat situations over the years and was twice awarded gallantry medals. His men looked up to this hero, as did his superiors. He, on his part never failed to give correct operational advice, even at the expense of disagreement with superiors, if required. That is what made him so invaluable, especially when it is a matter of life and death.

Lieutenant Colonel Sean also adjusted the other ambushes accordingly and sent one additional patrol to lay another ambush in the killing area. Their D Company was deployed on the extreme flank of the battalion and further to the west was the neighbouring brigade. Coordination at the inter-formation boundary was always a tricky issue. But this Param Vir Chakra Paltan had such a great history of valour and glory that all soldiers were determined to succeed against all odds.

Now came the tricky part. After all readjustments and resisting were done and additional ambushes deployed, all they had to do was wait patiently—without making any noise, lest the infiltrating terrorists get a warning of their presence and change their route or turn back. That is the reason why laying an ambush is considered the trickiest operation. One small sound, a cough, the crackle of a radio set, even a muffled torchlight can alert the enemy, in this case the terrorists. Moreover, you are sitting in the open without any cover or protection, exposing yourself to hostile fire. You require nerves of steel. This is where good training and high motivation kicks in. Naib Subedar Chunni and his soldiers were exemplary in their operational conduct. They held their positions in complete silence and stillness. They were confident of getting the terrorists with such a head start. Their morale was high.

Suddenly, a thick fog started descending on them. This was pure bad luck. Fog favours the infiltrators and blinds soldiers waiting to ambush. Gradually the visibility dropped to a few yards. Chunni Lal put his radio set on 'squelch' mode[19] and whispered to his Company Commander only one word, 'Fog.'

Just when he had started getting confident of success, thought Sean now feeling disheartened. From his company HQ, he called the neighbouring Company Commander, Maj. Manoj Deshpande, VrC for reinforcements. It was the LORROS detachment at Manoj's company HQ location that had observed the movement of terrorists and hence, he had been keeping himself abreast of the developments. Manoj was a brave officer and had been in numerous combat situations in earlier tenures and was a gallantry awardee. In fact, he and Nb Sub. Chunni were awarded Vir Chakras together for an operation seven years earlier.

'I've already got two ambush parties ready in anticipation,' replied Manoj, 'but we have Chunni on the spot. He's the best we have.'

That is the kind of faith the officers of the battalion had in Chunni. He exuded an aura of invincibility.

'Move your men now,' said Sean. 'The fog is getting thicker. We need more troops to ensure that they don't escape in this dense fog. And I want your men to cover the south of road as well, an effective block just in case they make a dash southward.'

'Aye aye, Sir,' quipped Manoj, having picked up this Navy style of acknowledgement while serving with the Navy in the Andaman and Nicobar Islands, 'I'm coming along too. You didn't think I'd miss any chance of such action, did you?' They were old friends of over a decade and had served in different tenures together, not only in combat, but also including Sudan and Port Blair.

There was another ambush party ahead, code-named Cheetah. It was closer to where they expected the terrorists' route to lead them. However, the Cheetah team was unable to communicate, as their line communication was cut (and could only be repaired in the morning) nor were they responding on the radio set. Chunni volunteered to go across to warn them and co-ordinate. This was a great quality of his. Instead of deputing someone as the post commander, he wanted to take the risk himself. 'I'll also be able to co-ordinate my area of responsibility better,' he told Sean. He crawled forward with three soldiers including his buddy, silently, ghost-like. In such situations, even a loud rustle can mean the different between life and death.

However, Chunni and his boys were on the edge. By this time that terrorists should have reached their location. The worry was that they could use the cover of fog to escape unnoticed. Suddenly he heard some muffled sounds but could see nothing. They also could not make out the direction from where the sound had emanated. This is called the fog of war; nothing to do with the actual fog. He requested Sean to fire illuminating rounds from the rocket launcher, so that they could try to sight the terrorists if they were nearby. Two rounds of the 84 mm rocket launcher were fired and their hearts sank. The fog was even thicker than it seemed. It also seemed like an orange blur. It felt as if they were sitting in a cloud. It was also counterproductive.

They were no wiser, but the terrorists had been alerted that the soldiers knew of or suspected their presence.

So, Chunni decided to keep a keen ear to the ground, to hear the slightest sound of footsteps, breaking of a twig or any other giveaway. After what seemed to be eternity, although it was after a few minutes, he heard a sound. It was a short tap of metal against metal. He tensed. He heard it again after a few moments. Tik, Tik, Tik... went the sound after every few seconds. It was neither muffled, nor loud.

The sound was coming from the direction of the fence. He ordered opening of fire towards the sound. They fired the light machine guns and AK rifles. The noise of firing broke the stillness and suspense of the night. Although they were used to this noise every night, the soldiers found it extra loud tonight, perhaps a premonition of a good operation. The terrorists did not return fire. After a few minutes, Chunni ordered his soldiers to cease fire.

Day was about to break. Despite the fog, there would be some visibility.

Sean and his party were about to reach the site, when they heard the firing and Chunni briefed him about it on the radio set. Though Manoj's party was also on the way from another flank, but he also heard the brief on the radio set. That is the advantage of radio sets. All sets on the same frequency can hear all communications. But only one outstation can speak at a time. So, although he heard it, Manoj was careful not to make a comment, lest it clutter the frequency. While still on the move, Sean asked Manoj to despatch another patrol south of the road to reinforce our ambushes there due to poor visibility. This is called thickening of the ambushes.

On the reverse slope of the Shamshabari Range, there ran a road laterally that connected the company posts and the Battalion HQ. The terrorists aimed to cross the crest line, cut through the fence and reach south of the road before they were daylighted. The Army endeavoured to track them using night-vision equipment, hoping to ambush them at or before the fence, but certainly not letting them escape beyond the killing area between the fence and the road.

The anti-infiltration fence is not just a wire fence. It is a double fence, 12 feet high, and between the two fences, there are two concertina coils. There are sensors and lights depending on the threat perception and other improvised obstacles. The soldiers also tie empty bottles and empty tin cans so that it makes extra noise when terrorists attempt to cut the fence in darkness or poor visibility. If they still manage to cut through, even if they are wounded in firing by soldiers, our troops get them between the fence and the road. If a breach is detected in the fence, then the troops home on to the route that the terrorists have taken, rather than cover a wide area. They thicken the ambushes in the desired area to neutralize them. Hence it is called the killing area.

Soon it was first light, something Chunni had been impatiently waiting for. However, it did not bring much joy, as visibility continued to remain restricted because of the fog. He took a patrol of eight soldiers who were waiting with him, to check if there had been a breach in the fence. They crawled with caution, moving tactically, one leg on the ground. This means that when a few soldiers move, the others take position to guard against the suspected enemy. When the moving troops reach some distance they take position, and others move up from behind. The fog was still thick, favouring the terrorists, thus they had to exercise extreme caution.

Meanwhile in addition to Manoj's team, two more patrols had been deployed to cover the killing ground between the fence and the road. Chunni and his men moved cautiously—walking stealthily, crouching, crawling—depending on the terrain and the trees or the undergrowth. They could not afford to alert the terrorists about their advance or it could be fatal for them, but they could certainly not let them escape into the hinterland to cause more violence. Chunni was prepared for the first eventuality, it was an occupational hazard, but they could not let the second happen. That was unacceptable, especially after having discerned that the infiltrating terrorists had indeed cut through the fence from their area of responsibility.

Chunni felt personally responsible. That is the problem with an over-developed conscience, it flagellates itself unduly harshly. It was not acceptable to Chunni, as a responsible junior leader and a seasoned veteran of many combat situations. He would rather die than let them get through. This was his train of thought while moving forward tactically along the nallah. But they saw no sign of the terrorists. There was another ambush party deployed closer to the road. When he reached them, he connected with Nb Sub. Rajesh, the ambush commander. He assured them that the terrorists had not come their way.

'For how long have you personally been on duty?' Nb Sub. Chunni asked Nb Sub. Rajesh.

'For over two hours, brother, and I can assure you that they have not crossed my ambush, nor will they ever be allowed to.' Every soldier takes so much pride in their duty and responsibility. That made it worse for Chunni. He became sure that the terrorists were between the fence and the road and was determined to get them. At any cost.

So, he decided to move his patrol upwards almost tracing their steps towards the fence, but moving deeper inside the nallah where there was thick undergrowth. There were clumps of juniper-like bushes. It was risky, but he decided to risk it. Who knows behind which bush a terrorist might be lurking. Their movement upward was much slower, and it was not only due to the ascending altitude.

With his tactical sense and soldierly tracking instinct honed over years of combat experience, Chunni homed on to a dense thicket and undergrowth. That he had zeroed in to the correct spot, was confirmed by the fire they immediately drew.

He dived to the ground and rolled on to a side. He did not have to order his men to do the same. They did so reflexively. In any case, in such situations, there is no time to give orders. A moment's delay can mean the difference between life and death. A soldier's training kicks in reflexively in such situations. He re-sited his men and himself crawled to a flank and they returned fire at the terrorists in controlled bursts. The idea was to gauge their exact location and strength, judging from where all they were drawing fire.

By now Sean's party was below the road and they got pinned down by the terrorists' firing. Manoj's party was on one flank mercifully, and closing in fast. Manoj established a fire base with an automatic grenade launcher (AGL) and other weapons, on a little bump in the ground, giving him a positional advantage. Once Sean and his buddy moved a bit to adjust position, they were fired upon. Manoj's party saw this and immediately brought down effective fire of the AGL on the terrorists. It may not have hit the terrorists directly, but being an area weapon, it suppressed their movements effectively.

Chunni took stock of the situation hurriedly. His party was the only one in direct contact with the terrorists. The rest could only act as stops if a terrorist tried to flee the cordon. He lobbed a grenade and himself rolled down to a side on the lower slope to escape being hit by the shrapnel when the grenade exploded. One terrorist tried to dart out from the other side but Manoj's party brought down effective fire and he darted right back inside the thicket. A few rocks there gave some cover and protection to the terrorists.

The firing between Chunni's men and terrorists grew intense.

You have to draw a judicious balance between ammunition expenditure and firing enough so that terrorists are not able to break contact. That calls for seasoned combat experience, and Chunni had loads of it. Suddenly, one of his boys shouted. Chunni could make out Ranjit's voice. Though he could not hear well over the noise of shooting bullets, deep in his heart he knew that Ranjit was hit. He crawled closer under cover of undergrowth and gave a low shout, 'Oye, what happened?'

'Saabji, Ranjit is hit,' he heard a reply.

'Serious?'

'No, Sir, bullet wound in foot.'

'Thank God.'

'Keep firing the rest of you,' he said, 'I'll take care of him.'

Saying this, he crawled towards where Ranjit was still firing. While he was moving and firing alternately, he heard another shout. Tarsem was also hit. He decided they were too close and decided to evacuate the two wounded soldiers first. With the help of another soldier he pulled them to safety one by one. Thank God their wounds would not be fatal, although the bleeding was serious. They tied first field dressing (FFD), which helped to staunch the blood flow, albeit not completely. Satisfied that they would hold, Chunni turned his attention to the task at hand.

He was enraged. Two of his boys were hit. What if they were critical? Chunni couldn't bear the thought. A soldier laying down his life on your watch weighs heavily on any commander's shoulders and heart. Enraged he crawled forward, lobbed another grenade and then charged like a man possessed into the thicket before anyone could either stop him or accompany him.

There was a fierce and intense exchange of fire. Chunni fired like a madman as he burst on three crouching figures, his Kalashnikov AK 47 Rifle blazing. The terrorists also fired back, but he was quicker and knocked off the three of them. However, he was also hit. He felt the thud of a bullet in his bulletproof jacket. It nearly knocked the wind out of him, but kept him safe. Soon he was also hit in the stomach below the bulletproof jacket, and then in his groin. He knelt down, then lay down, fingers still on the trigger.

In utmost pain, he managed to turn his rifle towards the neighbouring thicket, from where more terrorists were still firing, although at a slower rate. Slowly, life was ebbing out of him. He tried to focus his eyes. He did not utter any sound. That was typical of him. In his heart he had the satisfaction of knowing that he did not let terrorists escape from his area of responsibility towards the hinterland to cause violence on his brethren, or worse still, on innocent civilians. He must've thought about his family, but he accepted his end calmly, as the most honourable way to go for a soldier—by facing a bullet from the front and being successful in his mission.

Both Sean and Manoj sensed that the firefight was at a climax. When Sean's party closed in from one side and Manoj's team from another, the firing was low. The other two terrorists had also been wounded by Nb Sub. Chunni's onslaught.

They did a quick mopping up, ensuring that no terrorists were left alive. What may seem peculiar to the reader is that the mission comes first, and even a wounded comrade will understand that they'll tend to him later. Having satisfied themselves that the area was secure, when they reached where Chunni was lying they turned him over. His face was surprisingly calm, as if satisfied as a soldier that he had not let the infiltrators through on his watch.

There was an air of disbelief in the unit. Naib Subedar Chunni Lal had an aura of invincibility. He had always been a reassuring factor in combat situations. His mere presence in operations would reassure superiors and subordinates alike. Earlier that night, when infiltrators had been spotted, Lt Col Sean had asked Maj. Manoj on telephone if they should be taking some more actions to ensure success. Major Manoj had simply said, 'We've sent our fail-safe combat machine, Chunni, what more?' That was the amount of confidence that the whole unit had in him.

Naib Subedar Chunni Lal was given a simple but a hero's farewell. There was not a heart in the unit that did not feel heavy. Although death is an occupational hazard in the profession of arms, and is taken more stoically in operational units, but there was not a soul in the unit whose heart did not feel heavy at the passing of this hero. Several soldiers cried openly and many confined themselves to moist eyes. Such was the aura of this great soldier.

Naib Subedar Chunni had come to symbolize reassurance, in operations. His superiors felt reassured of a positive result in any operation that he was participating in. His subordinates felt his reassuring presence to be a touchstone of faith—that no misfortune could befall them and victory would be theirs. So compelling was his presence, that no one ever thought that something could happen to him. Though awarded gallantry medals only thrice, he had participated in countless operations and deserved many more, but he would himself say, 'I already have medals, others bravery should be recognized.'

A wreath laying is normally followed by soldiers going home accompanied by a close friend or two from his village or region.

Suresh took him home for the last time. How apt. They both started their journey in the Army and JAKLI together. It was so apt that he accompanied Chunni on the hero's last journey home.

A grateful nation conferred upon this bravest of the brave son of the soil, the highest gallantry award that is awarded during peace time, the Ashok Chakra.

Having an eye for the ground, locating the right man at the right place in an ambush, opening fire on the terrorists when detected, at the right time—not early, not late—are the key factors, and vital for survival. The terrorist will kill you if you don't kill him first. If you open fire when he is still out of your effective range, he will run away and escape. Therefore, a judicious balance had to be drawn on when to fire.

That is the reason why laying an ambush is considered the trickiest operation. One small sound, a cough, the crackle of a radio set, even a muffled torchlight can alert the enemy, in this case the terrorists. Moreover, you are sitting in the open without any cover or protection, exposing yourself to hostile fire. You require nerves of steel. This is where good training and high motivation kicks in.

Afterword

NAIB SUBEDAR CHUNNI Lal was awarded three among the four highest gallantry awards of the Indian Army—the Ashok Chakra, Vir Chakra and Sena Medal. He is the only soldier in the Indian Army to hold this distinction. This has found mention in the *Limca Book of Records*. What is also remarkable is the fact that he received these awards in an ascending order. It is also interesting to note that the operations for which he received these awards were in all three regions of the erstwhile J&K state (now a union territory minus Ladakh), namely the Ashok Chakra in Kupwara in Kashmir region, Vir Chakra in Poonch in Jammu region, and the Sena Medal at the Siachen Glacier in Ladakh region. He was a true son of the soil.

With the award of Ashok Chakra to Naib Subedar Chunni Lal, 8th Battalion, Jammu and Kashmir Light Infantry or 8 JAKLI (Siachen), was conferred the title, 'Bravest of the Brave', a rare and a coveted honour granted to very few select units which have won two of the highest awards, Param Vir Chakra and/or Ashok Chakra.

Subedar Major and Honorary Captain Bana Singh had been awarded the Param Vir Chakra for the highest attack in the world exactly twenty years prior to Naib Subedar Chunni Lal's supreme sacrifice and what's more, Chunni was a part of that operation also as a rookie soldier and earned his first award, the Sena Medal, then. Bana Singh once told me, 'In his first operation, despite his young age, Chunni displayed no fear. I was confident even then that he had the makings of a great soldier.'

Lieutenant General Sami Khan, PVSM, SM, had held a special Sainik Sammelan as the Corps Commander, while congratulating the battalion for the stupendous operations executed by the battalion at the Siachen Glacier. As mentioned earlier in this book, he had said, '*Yeh toh devtaaon ka kaam hai, jo aap sab ne kar dikhaya hai.*' (It is the work of the gods that you all have managed to do). Naib Subedar Chunni was a part of that final attack as a young rookie soldier. Now, he is among the angels.

'*Voh dekh raha hai,*' (He is watching) as the trainees in OTA say while speaking of his statue, his bust installed at the Parade ground there.

A few years after Chunni left us, our Paltan was selected to be posted as the Presidents Infantry Guard in Rashtrapati Bhavan in 2014. It was a rare honour. During one of my visit to the unit (I was posted in Army HQ as a Maj. Gen. then) it struck me that had Chunni been alive, he would have been introduced to all Indian and foreign dignitaries, including heads of state. He may even have been uncomfortable. But in our battalion's next tenure, which was in Sunderbani, which was the very same location on the LoC where we had won two Battle Honours (Laleali and Picquet 707) and several gallantry medals in 1971, Chunni would have been a great asset, a

Afterword

source of inspiration and above all his chest would have swelled with pride to serve in the same place where our battalion's operational history was legendary.

Talking of the 1971 operations of our battalion, I reminisced that Hony Capt. Bana was a rookie soldier in the 1971 war, earned his spurs in the 1971 war, and was eventually awarded the Param Vir Chakra. Hav. Chunni Lal was a rookie in the Siachen Glacier operations, and eventually awarded the Ashok Chakra. Both heroes had been baptized by fire.

His son, Manveer, carries forward his father's proud legacy by serving in the same Bravest of the Brave Battalion. I recall fondly that I went to attend his daughter's wedding in 2016, when I was the Corps Commander of the Srinagar based 15 Corps. I had to go by a chopper up to a helipad in the mountainous areas of Bhaderwah, from there by a dirt track by a Gypsy and finally walk up for twenty odd minutes to his village. But it gave me great satisfaction to attend his daughter's wedding. One year after my retirement, I went on a motorcycle to his village, when his bust was being installed in a park named after him. Such are the bonds of brotherhood in the army.

Naib Subedar Chunni Lal, AC, VrC, SM, continues to inspire generations of soldiers. Some of us were fortunate to serve with him in combat and otherwise. For me, it was a matter of a proud privilege that I had been his commanding officer as well. I learnt a lot from him.

A National Salute to the Bravest of the Brave.

Jai Hind.

Hony Capt. Bana was a rookie soldier in the 1971 war and earned his spurs in the 1971 war, and was eventually awarded the Param Vir Chakra.

Hav. Chunni Lal was a rookie in the Siachen Glacier operations, and eventually awarded the Ashok Chakra. Both heroes had been baptized by fire.

Acknowledgements

My father would always urge me to write a book, even when I was busy soldiering. Just like my earlier books, this one is also for you, Dad. You have always been my role model.

I seek the blessings of Sri Aurobindo and the Divine Mother for this book as well as for everything else.

I want to acknowledge the role of my wife, Aradhana, and my sons, Adamya and Ardaman, who put up with my absence from home for years at a stretch, owing to my deployments in operational areas, the experience of which enabled me to write this book.

Nb Sub. Chunni Lal and I have served together in combat and peace, but to piece together the story of the times when we were not together, I have interviewed many officers and soldiers of my own battalion. To learn about his childhood and family life, I have travelled to his village twice and met his family, relatives and friends.

It may not be possible to acknowledge everyone by name, but I would like to thank the more prominent ones, and several of the rest appear in the narrative. I wish to begin by profusely thanking the parents and wife, Mrs Chinta Devi, of Nb Sub. Chunni Lal, his close buddies, Hony Capt. Laxman Dass, VrC and Hony Capt.

Suresh Chand for their insights, as also his seniors like Hony Capt. Sansar Chand, MVC, Hony Capt. Bana Singh, PVC and Hony Capt. Balwant Singh, VrC. (This reads like an impressive gallantry medals list, and it makes me proud). A special thanks to Hav. Manveer Singh, son of Nb Sub. Chunni Lal, AC, VrC, SM, for giving me his understanding of his father as a parent and as a soldier. I used to refer back to him for all queries, especially as he is still serving proudly in our Bravest of the Brave Battalion.

I also thank Brig. R.E. Williams (I have also quoted from his book, *A Long Road to Siachen*), Col R.K. Singh, Col Rajiv Maithani and Lt Col Anil Sharma, all from my battalion, for their insights into the operations at the Siachen Glacier.

My gratitude goes out to Late Maj. Gen Anil Malik for his insight as the CO, 2 JAKLI in Somalia and Brig. Bharat Shekhawat for his insight as our CO in Sudan; from them I gleaned Chunni's role and performance in UN peacekeeping missions.

I also thank Col Manoj Deshpande, Lt Col Sean O'Brien and Lt Col Himanshu Sawant for their insights into the numerous counter terrorist operations that Chunni participated in, including his last encounter, where he made the supreme sacrifice and was awarded Ashok Chakra (posthumously).

I also warmly thank my publisher and editor, Udayan Mitra, for his expert guidance through the writing of this book. I also express my gratitude for the team at Harper Collins comprising Shreya Mukherjee, Sashi Aiyer and Amit Malhotra.

Finally, I thank all my mentors and superiors, the brave officers and soldiers that I have been fortunate to command, not only in my Bravest of the Brave Battalion, 8 JAKLI (Siachen), but also beyond, throughout my career, for I have learned something from everyone.

I also thank the reader for being a part of this journey now.

Jai Hind!

Notes

1. Col (later Brig.) S.C. Katoch was the CO of the Battalion who composed this song in the mid-seventies. At that time, the highest awards the battalion had were four Vir Chakras—one in the 1948 operations and three in the Indo–Pak war of 1971.
2. A company consists of around 120 soldiers, who form this basic fighting unit. It is commanded by a Major, who had the command of three platoons of around thirty-five men each.
3. The altitude at the Siachen Glacier ranges between 11,713 to 20,062 feet. Source: https://www.britannica.com/place/Siachen-Glacier.

    Humans are able to breathe comfortably without supplemental oxygen at 8,000 feet and below.
4. However, the mountain peaks on which the Army is deployed is on the Saltoro Ridge which looms above the glacier and is considerably higher. The crest of the Saltoro Ridge's altitudes range from 17,880 feet to 25,330 feet). Source: https://en.wikipedia.org/wiki/Siachen_Glacier
5. Temperatures are given in Celsius throughout.
6. Rifleman (Rfn) is the rank of a soldier. He is called Sepoy (Sep) in rest of the army, but in Light Infantry and Rifle Regiments he is referred to as 'Rfn'.

7. When troops are deployed at high altitude areas, soldiers have to follow an acclimatization plan as described in the text. First stage is at 9,000 feet for six days, second stage is at 12,000 feet for four days and third stage is at 15,000 feet for four days.
8. Since those days, the Army has acquired biodigesters, in which bacteria is used to convert biodegradable waste into manure.
9. 2Lt Rajiv Pandey was the patrol leader. In generic terms 2Lt are referred to as Lt, just like Lt Gen. or Maj. Gen. are referred to as Gen.
10. A Saddle is the little trough between two mountain peaks.
11. Williams, Brig. Rajiv, and Verma, Kunal, *The Long Road to Siachen: The Question Why*, New Delhi: Rupa Publications Ltd, 2010.
12. Training courses are conducted at Army training schools, training cadres are conducted at unit level.
13. While it is not the national currency, US dollars were widely used in Somalia then.
14. The 'interview' refers to the 'CO's Interview', which is regularly held and is an interview of the men with the CO. Those called for the interview line up for the interview parade.
15. A reentrant is a small valley-like formation in a hillside that appears as a U or V shape on a map. Reentrants are characterized by three sides that slope upwards and one side that slopes downwards.
16. From the poem 'The Sea Shell' by William Wordsworth.
17. In 2011, South Sudan separated from Sudan and declared itself an independent nation. The two countries are now known as Sudan and South Sudan. This book refers to pre-2007 times, when the two were still one nation.
18. In Sudan, the UN Forces were assigned sectors, equivalent to area of responsibility.
19. In squelch mode, a radio set becomes completely silent (the sound of static is silenced). However, it consumes more battery and, thus, has to be used sparingly.

About the Author

Lieutenant General Satish Dua, PVSM, UYSM, SM, VSM, retired as Chief of Integrated Defence Staff in 2018. In response to the terror attack at Uri, Kashmir, in 2016, he planned and executed the surgical strikes as Corps Commander in Srinagar. A counter-terrorism specialist from 8 JAKLI (Siachen), he has operated extensively in Jammu and Kashmir and the Northeast during his four decades of service. As Chief of Integrated Defence Staff, he steered the construction of the National War Memorial. He has also served as a Commando Instructor, and India's Defence Attaché in Vietnam, Cambodia and Laos.

HarperCollins *Publishers* India

At HarperCollins India, we believe in telling the best stories and finding the widest readership for our books in every format possible. We started publishing in 1992; a great deal has changed since then, but what has remained constant is the passion with which our authors write their books, the love with which readers receive them, and the sheer joy and excitement that we as publishers feel in being a part of the publishing process.

Over the years, we've had the pleasure of publishing some of the finest writing from the subcontinent and around the world, including several award-winning titles and some of the biggest bestsellers in India's publishing history. But nothing has meant more to us than the fact that millions of people have read the books we published, and that somewhere, a book of ours might have made a difference.

As we look to the future, we go back to that one word—a word which has been a driving force for us all these years.

Read.